# WILLOW ROOM, GREEN DOOR

Also by
DEBORAH KEENAN

—

*Kingdoms*

*Good Heart*

*Happiness*

*The Only Window That Counts*

*How We Missed Belgium* (with Jim Moore)

*One Angel Then*

*Household Wounds*

# WILLOW ROOM, GREEN DOOR

## NEW AND SELECTED POEMS

Deborah Keenan

MILKWEED EDITIONS

Published 2007 by Milkweed Editions
Printed in Canada
Cover design by Christian Fuenfhausen
Cover photo of willow tree flower by istockphoto.com/AVTG
Author photo by Emily Cook
Interior design by Christian Fuenfhausen
Typeset by Dorie McClelland, Spring Book Design
The text of this book is set in Goudy Old Style BT.
07 08 09 10 11  5 4 3 2 1
*First Edition*

Milkweed Editions, a nonprofit publisher, gratefully acknowledges sustaining support from Emilie and Henry Buchwald; the Bush Foundation; the Patrick and Aimee Butler Family Foundation; CarVal Investors; the Timothy and Tara Clark Family Charitable Fund; the Dougherty Family Foundation; the Ecolab Foundation; the General Mills Foundation; the Claire Giannini Fund; John and Joanne Gordon; William and Jeanne Grandy; the Jerome Foundation; Dorothy Kaplan Light and Ernest Light; Constance B. Kunin; Marshall BankFirst Corp.; Sanders and Tasha Marvin; the May Department Stores Company Foundation; the McKnight Foundation; a grant from the Minnesota State Arts Board, through an appropriation by the Minnesota State Legislature, a grant from the National Endowment for the Arts, and private funders; an award from the National Endowment for the Arts, which believes that a great nation deserves great art; the Navarre Corporation; Debbie Reynolds; the St. Paul Travelers Foundation; Ellen and Sheldon Sturgis; the Target Foundation; the Gertrude Sexton Thompson Charitable Trust (George R. A. Johnson, Trustee); the James R. Thorpe Foundation; the Toro Foundation; Moira and John Turner; United Parcel Service; Joanne and Phil Von Blon; Kathleen and Bill Wanner; Serene and Christopher Warren; the W. M. Foundation; and the Xcel Energy Foundation.

Deborah Keenan, "Small History," "Alone," "Architecture," "The Fathers Walking Away from Houses," "When the Dead Come to Visit in Dreams," "Fox," "Living," "Burning," "Loving Motels," "Rogue Wave," "Why They Belong Together," "Comfort," "What It Was Like Today," "Lilacs and Hail," "Night Walk," "Amnesia Plague," "How I Walk," and "Cordelia: One Portrait at a Time" from *Happiness*. Copyright © 1995 by Deborah Keenan. Reprinted with the permission of Coffee House Press, www.coffeehousepress.org.

Library of Congress Cataloging-in-Publication Data

Keenan, Deborah.
      Willow Room, green door : new and selected poems / Deborah Keenan.
            p. cm.
    ISBN 978-1-57131-426-0 (pbk. : alk. paper)
    ISBN 1-57131-426-1 (pbk. : alk. paper)
    1. Title
    PS3561.E36W55 2007
    811'.54–DC22

                        2006033339

This book is printed on acid-free,
recycled (100% post-consumer waste) paper.

NATIONAL
ENDOWMENT
FOR THE ARTS
A great nation
deserves great art.

MINNESOTA
STATE ARTS BOARD

*For my family,*
*past, present, future.*
*For my friends, and for my students*
*who keep the lamps lit as they read and write.*

———————

# WILLOW ROOM, GREEN DOOR

## WILLOW ROOM, GREEN DOOR

### I

### II

### III

# HOUSEHOLD WOUNDS

# ONE ANGEL THEN

# THE ONLY WINDOW THAT COUNTS

# HAPPINESS

# GOOD HEART

# KINGDOMS

# WILLOW ROOM,
# GREEN DOOR

# WILLOW ROOM, GREEN DOOR

I

# The Beauty of the Painting

That she hadn't ruined it      as steward was not found
Wanting      many other things were destroyed
The painting rested on the wooden floor
In the willow room      unharmed it offered a way
Out

# THE EXACTNESS
## OF THE IMITATION

It was a path through woods at dusk
Anyone could understand      anyone could
Get up from the table and walk on the path

# THE APPROPRIATENESS
# OF THE DEPICTION

This small painting she kept in her home.
Private. No judgments by others,
No door. Just the path.
It seemed appropriate. Forest. Yes.
Dusk—that word he loved so much. Yes.
Path. That was the problem, of course.
The journey, sensed as almost over,
Suddenly needing more thought.
The long view, now seen as worthless
Or at least     not helpful to anyone.
Who had trained her for the long view?

Was there even a house in the painting?
And knowing she would never live
In a yellow house yet had once said yes
To a house of Kandinsky's—
His sense of yellow inviting, correct.

# Verlag Dabritz, Long Ago in Munich, Now in the Poem

Adding his seasonal paintings was only about joy.
Benevolent Grandma Moses but a man. His joy
Different than Grandma's. Not labeled *outsider*
He could stay inside and paint the onion domes
Near the prancing brown horse, the beautiful
Pure white cows that made her weep.

Oh, the ideal colors of animals, though
The museum she knew and walked in decided to prove
Its VALUE—its hipness quotient—by not hanging Marc's
Blue horses. She understood now that she
Was on strike, though the two young people
She loved wandered the Sculpture Garden
At night      (they were two together, body and soul)
Though the two were thought too young
To truly love she had a weird faith in them—

So far on her path, the journey set, or not,
Still—not displaying Marc's blue horses—
She was finally old enough and smart enough
To register the loss, to turn away from the not-
Glistening-enough exterior. And since she
Could no longer cross Armajani's bridge

(Old memory, Annemarie and Cordelia
Holding her hands, walking her across the bridge
In blazing sunlight (not dusk), she kept her eyes
Closed and tears leaked out—she knew Ashbery's
Poem was going by at her feet and could not read it)

Since she could not cross, she kept the glass fish
Safe in her mind, kept Butterfield's tormented
Horse safe in her mind, kept the two who were
Thought too young to truly love safe in her mind,
Kept Franz Marc and his beloved animals, all
Safe in her mind.

She had spent a life in private protest
And what good had it ever done?

And Dabritz—what of his joy? His paintings? She didn't
Want to mention him as decoration. His burnt orange.
His gentle white cows. His brown horse
Wearing a coat of many colors
As miniature grown-ups full of joy (his joy?
Their joy) made a world in the snow.

# The Game In Progress

Mortal man and devil in disguise.
Baby-faced neuter angel watching
As the chessboard erupts into
Little white skulls, then a field
Of crosses and rosaries.

Has this game been won or lost?
The artist so committed to his iconography
He never needed an audience.

Peaceful, she thought. She thought:
*Oh, this is how I like to torment myself*
*On summer mornings.* Make the list
Of those who are sure of themselves,
Make the list from that list of those
Who have broken something inside her
That she used to call spirit, she used to call
God and beauty.

Take the word VALUES away from the sure ones.
Return it to the painters.

# Still Life with Scapegoat //
# Safe in the Family

The scapegoat in the wilderness looks proud
And lonely, too. It's an etching—the fine lines
The engraver loved, the pressure it caused
Inside his strong wrist as he pressed down
Again and again. This scapegoat is ancient
And bemused. Sins tied around his shaggy neck,
Driven from the village, the tap, tap, tap
Of his cloven hoofs on the hard rock
Of the mountain ridges. So there he is,
And chews off the bundle (goat version
Of Bunyan's parable moment)
And he's free of sin again, as he ever was.
But alone. Can he go back
To the village? Would he wish to?

In the still-life family she's created
There's enormous safety, huge allowance,
Since all in the still-life
Family are other. Two neutral angels
Flown in from Guatemala by Rosie,
Who stand guard and
Are of the family. Next to them, Gardening

Angel from Laurie, old white man but like
Priests and other pretend and real holy ones
He's cloaked in a garment that refuses to define
Sex. Then historical, white John Smith,
But in miniature, diminished and proud,
Standing on a small box decorated with
Pansies she'd given her mom in a Christmas
Stocking one year. John Smith who for years
Was part of a party game her youngest
Had invented for birthdays—so small he
Could be flipped into glasses full of juice
Or pop, float to the surface, be rescued
Over and over (all the little girls pretending
To be Pocahontas) then finally perched on
Top of whatever cake, his arms folded
In peace. John stands next to Little Peppy,
Wooden pepper shaker from the fifties,
A rotund maybe-girl/maybe-boy
To be shaken in honor of taste.
And the Russian maiden painted on
A shining miniature black box—in
The family in honor of her best friend.
In the family in honor of how much
The Russian maiden looks like
Country Maiden painted so long
Ago by Ryder—one of the few
Canvases saved to show his brilliant
Visions—

(Her love for Ryder dug at her some days—
She might stare at Berthot and dream of Ryder,

She might think of him saying to a friend,
After years of work on a single painting,
*The sky is getting interesting*)

And the Russian maiden stands
By five dice, cream and white and yellow,
All their lucky, neutral marks still visible,
The dice part of the family in honor of
Luck and fate, then the scapegoat—

Safe in the family—that was her decision.
No bundle of sin tied to his neck. No
Being sent away in honor of someone else's
Mistake or error or wickedness. This scapegoat
Golden, the color of the lions she loved.
Embraced by the family as they lived their
Lives in window light. A Christmas ago
Her oldest son had sent her the Elf doll.
She'd wanted to see the movie, wanted to hear
Will Ferrell say to the false Santa, "You sit
On a throne of lies!" so Elf arrived bubble-
Wrapped. He was the kind of toy that's
Not really a toy. If you pinched his back
His clasped hands would open. So she pinched
His back—he offered his small embrace
To the still-life family, and the two
Guatemalan angels made room for him
In the winter sunlight.

# II

# The Complete and Undisturbed Lion Skeleton

Rosie handed her the article because lion references were key. "Maybe the lion's importance is as a family pet rather than as a representative of a god." The first lion mummy was found in the tomb of King Tut's wet nurse. Years ago she wrote a long poem about the Greenland mummy, and one famous author sighed as she sat down after reading it, and remembered her name for one night, and clasped her left shoulder, the shoulder where she kept her power, and said, *brilliant*. She decided to live on that word for a few months; it kept her from her own impoverished feelings. The archeologists always sound brilliant in articles—this is true. "It confirms the status of the lion as a sacred animal." Is this really what we all were waiting for to confirm this idea? She doesn't think so. Raggedy gold lions are sacred in so many cultures; they may have taken over for the gods long before the first myths were written. She is disturbed. The violent summer wind she loves is not a comfort tonight. She broods about lions and lives in the city, afraid of raccoons and rats—she considers the life in the sewer system under her city and has a panic attack—private and almost serene in her fear. They say the lion mummy is artifact, not art. She thinks: all lions wrapped in shrouds of linen, resting with their heads on the breasts of wet nurses—all these lions are art, even if there's only one.

# Guessed "True" Answer Was "Bridge"

Not the bridge she can no longer cross, Ashbery's words at her feet. Not Stirling Bridge, her first child inside her, faithfully painting its beautiful arc and curve over and over again. Not the newer bridges over Nine Mile Creek, not even the one where she lay on her back staring up into the cloudless blue sky praying never to leave. The lost bridge, the one torn away by the spring flood, the bridge that is the true answer. It is clear now, taking the long view, that the bridge could never have been repaired. She hopes now to never write of her creek again, sees how it both is her spiritual work, and hinders her spiritual work. Her mother made a painting of this particular curve of the creek—she remembers her mother coming home from her first painting class, her mother longing to be an artist like her sister Marjorie, her sisters-in-law Helen and Lorretta. How could the girl tell the mother it would never happen? She could not tell her. The curve of the creek was done in mud brown paint—her mother had honored the teacher who said, *don't paint it as you imagine it, paint it as it is.* Her mother painted the curve of water, skipped the bridge, added twenty dark brown trunks of trees. She kept her mother's painting in her garage for twenty-one years. Then she threw it away. Somehow that painting got connected with cleaning out the old garage before it would be knocked down for a new garage. Her shame as her husband found thing after thing after thing she had been saving for too many years. So she saved the broken pieces of her father's handmade bird feeders, but threw away the last of the Christmas ornaments and her mother's painting. She once had plans, needed the dream of the made thing in front of her every day. Has anything changed? She always had those kinds of plans—make the thing from the thing it no longer is. Make the collage about trains from broken bird feeders. Make the collage about the creek by using her mother's terrible creek. Make the children remember their grandmother by giving them bashed and broken Christmas ornaments they might or might not remember. Make the thing from the thing it no longer is. Her motto, cradle to grave.

III

# Maybe He's Grateful but Get Out of His Way

The Siberian tiger leaps from the back of the truck:
He'd been caught in a snare, rescued by Russian students
Deep in the forest, tranquilized, observed, fitted with a radio
Collar, woken up as if from a human dream for tigers,
Driven back to the forest, the cage opened, the leap,
And gone.

Four hundred left. Poachers demented with greed
Want every part of the Siberian tiger but never
The whole tiger.

# KANDINSKY IN THE HERMITAGE

The yellow house she had once agreed to live in was this one.
A double path of pink and blue, spotted with dots of lavender,
Led to the house, whose door could only be imagined—
Kandinsky loved the four small black windows,
The yellow sky outlining the mountains. Her oldest
Daughter had traveled to St. Petersburg with her oldest
Brother. Brought Kandinsky home—all Kandinsky
Postcards among the most beautiful of all postcards.

His spiritual life had sent her into delirium years ago.
*Winter* and *View of Murnau* made his soul visible.
It no longer mattered to her that his travels to abstraction
Were more revered by others in art history class.
She looked to early evidence
For revelation now, for beauty, too, and the meaning
Of beginning, of starting out.

# November 1, 2004

I carried a yellow leaf from my garden to Captiva Island
And matched its color to his yellow house. I drew
The leaf at six AM when the first osprey
Flew overhead, mouth jammed with seaweed.

# Passage from Isaiah

*He is . . . a man of sorrows, and acquainted with grief.*
Isaiah 53:3

November 4 was her father's birthday. He owned
This line from Isaiah. She did not want her sad father's
Birth day to be one day after her beautiful husband's
Birth day. In all her journals a tribute, a drawing,
A private moment of love for her husband on November 3,
Then you can turn the page, and she may or may not
Comment on her father's birthday.
(She has an old memory—*is it true?*—her oldest brother
Calling her mother every November 4.)

Then, certain Wallace Stevens lines
(Maybe *The spring clouds blow*
*Above the shuttered mansion-house,*
*Beyond our gate and the windy sky*
*Cries out a literate despair.*)
Combined with certain Shirley Jackson lines,
Perhaps: *There was a strong feeling of triumph and an odd feeling*
*of vengeance and once when she stopped under a tree and*
*leaned her head against its firm rough trunk she whispered softly,*
*"I know, I know."*

You can see the problem here. And so could she.

# Traveling in the Realms of Gold

Cordelia wrote: But I think of my family as royal. Princesses
    wear crowns to remind them they are beautiful and special.
    But I, Corey, am not a princess and I don't want to be.

She found this scrap of paper, as she'd found so many others.
She thought of Elvis Costello. *The angels wanna wear my red shoes.*

She understood this was the link. However, she could not bring
    it to completion.

# Research on the Color Red

Red shoes. (Add all mythic and historical evidence/old movie
    scripts/Jean's red sandals.)
Her dear friend Susan's powerful and uneasy relationship with
    red. Though she knows
Hummingbirds would come more easily to her fabulous garden if
    she would just
Plant the red verbena, the slender-throated red lilies, the hybrid
    traveling/swooping
Red petunias.
Molly's red wedding dress. Scarlet. Crimson. Brilliant in its cut
    and sound.
Brilliant as the tale of the single red lily in the garden trans-
    formed into beloved bride.
Other references to red found in previous six books. The
    mother's red hair, of course.
But much more research to be done. When she has time.

# IV

# It's a Book about Summer, So Cottonwoods and the Rivers Are Key

Cotton swamps the gutters, softens the sides of streets, after rain
Is carried down to the sewer system, for rats and raccoons—softens
The nests of the new ones beginning their lives in the dark.

The birds can't gather it fast enough—flight patterns precise
As they fly and swoop into the edges of all the east/west streets,
The north/south streets, their mouths crammed with cotton
And they lift off over and over again in the heat.

She grew up near an ancient creek bed, cottonwoods, the sweet
Smell of basswoods, lindens, oaks and old apple trees, elms
That towered and held the swinging Baltimore oriole nests.
Willows and birch, maples and lilacs. Every poet she knows
Who actually believes in the idea of making meaning
Lists the names of trees. Now that she is so much older
She understands all that she does as an artist that allows
Other artists to render her invisible. She
Is interested in how power works in her world. Why Cezanne
Wins every art brawl, why his edges aren't edges. Why
The poet who says *jacaranda* wins, and the poet who says

*lilac* loses. It's a book about summer, so the body count
In Iraq is key. It's a book about summer, so she has to listen
To leaders tell their white lies. She has to remember that
Forty-nine dead in London outweigh thousands of dead women,
Children, and men in Iraq and Afghanistan.

Cotton swamps the gutters. It is trying to soften everything,
Because the cottonwood knows its job. The river knows,
Too. And the poets, the painters, the soldiers. Everyone
Got up this morning and knew her job.

# Angel Island and Its Meaning and VALUE

As the ferryboats chug close to the island, ready to pick
Up the day-trippers, she sees the raccoons file down,
Vertical lines down the hills, five and six in each line,
Then they straighten to horizontal lines, masked and waiting
For the ferryboats to fill, so they can eat their fill of what
The humans have left behind—there's only one snack bar
But people know how to buy and eat and stop eating and toss
And raccoons know how to lift the french fries with their delicate
Paws, know how to lick the last of the melted cheese and broken
    chips
From the cardboard boat, graze and consume and be filled.
My friend wondered how they got to the island. After all the
    desperate,
Hopeful Asian people arrived,
Held on Angel Island until deemed fit for the mainland, until
    deemed fit
For the beautiful one-of-a-kind-experiment-in-democracy-
    America,
After all the immigrant dreams of a certain time saturated and
    defined

This island, then one pregnant raccoon set off swimming from
    the mainland,
Her mate by her side. They did the sidestroke until they reached
    the shore,
Then sent up flares for their friends to follow—they knew the
    danger
Of inbreeding. Angel Island a heavenly home in America for
    tourists
Who contemplate their luck and fate and french fries in the
    summer heat.

# THE BLACK ANGEL AND
# HENRI COULETTE

*Where are the people as beautiful as poems,*
*As calm as mirrors,*
*With their oceanic longings—*

After he wrote that the world seemed a little different,
And she didn't write for a couple of years.

Then he wrote, *I think of that friend too much moved by music*
*Who turned to games*
*And made a game of boredom,*
*Of that one too much moved by faces*
*Who turned his face to the wall, and of that marvelous liar*
*Who turned at last to truth.*

After that she made a collage and searched for the Black Angel.
She knew how Ashbery embedded his poems with the words
Of others. She wasn't an idiot about the food chain. After
She decided to write again, the Black Angel and Henri Coulette
Stayed with her, and Ashbery as always, along for the ride.

Perhaps Ryder was a guardian angel this time, or the beautiful
Young couple almost alone in the dark of the Sculpture Garden.
Maybe it was her oldest daughter, married to Aaron the last hours
Of April, maybe those two provided just enough protection for
    the poem
To be written.

Every book she wrote contained fewer lies. And every book
Was shorter. She thought of Joyce Carol Oates writing a novella.
The intensity of that choice, thought of jco running, slender
    and silent
With the book coming to life in her mind and footfalls. The book
    where people made decisions for life, where children walked
Into the hills carrying private lanterns.
Thought of Celan in his enormous suffering writing toward silence.
Thought of power and glory, of diminishing returns and closing
The poem down.

# V

## Woman on Laurel Street Reports That Her Neighbor Has Stolen Nine Pairs of Her Shoes and Left a Pile of Honey and Flour by Her Car

Her husband gave her a book: photos of concrete angels hidden in churches. The one she loves wears a wreath of primroses, has a perfect, naked foot showing, kneels on one knee, holds a giant basin chiseled into the shape of a scallop shell. The shell/basin is two feet across, so you can imagine the work of the wings when she wants to take off. Her foot is erotic, narrow and strong. She looks a lot like an angel from the summer of love—hair hanging down, the calm look of hope on her face. She assumes the creator is a woman, then a man—what kind of artist would want an angel just like this? She would.

The local paper reports that a woman has received a photograph in the mail—her snowman, stolen two nights before, with a machete in its throat and a knife in its eye. Police believe neighborhood children are responsible. It's summer, so now's a good time to think of this winter crime. A few months ago she told her youngest daughter that the next time there was a huge winter storm on a mild enough day, she would gather all her daughter's friends and drop them on the center land of the divided avenue—she told her that only a few years ago young people took the time to make extraordinary snow sculptures on the avenue: ten-foot rabbits holding snow baskets; a giant snow person with no gender, wearing a black velvet cape; a snow house big enough for a first-grade class to hide inside of. She is trying to inspire her daughter. She thinks some of her daughter's friends would put up with her wanting this. She thinks Francie would give her a loving smile, say yes. Maybe some others. She is full of dread too often about the future. Twenty-four Iraqi children blown up yesterday, with one American soldier, as he was handing them candy. She wants her daughter to go to the middle of the avenue and build something that cannot last.

# WOMAN ON BOTTICELLI STREET REPORTS THE PHRASE "THE END IS NEAR" WRITTEN IN WAX ON HER DRIVEWAY

In her twenties when she lived on Botticelli Street she kept reporting baby angels who turned out to be regular babies let loose by stymied, unhappy mothers in the early morning. These mothers trusted the strangers in the neighborhood to keep the babies safe until they could stand to be with them again. When she lived on Botticelli Street she reported seeing small golden lions sleeping in the boulevard gardens. When she lived on Botticelli Street she longed for the new millennium, for the end of war, and the beginning of a new art movement that would honor all that was small and precise. When she lived on Botticelli Street she wanted an end to video installations, voice-overs, and roadkill dressed in doll clothes and displayed inside glass boxes. When she lived on Botticelli Street she saw a cat dressed in a nurse's uniform run by. When she lived on Botticelli Street the only art that mattered to her was oil paintings, but she never felt much kinship with Gertrude Stein. When she lived on Botticelli Street most of the babies set loose by their mothers in the early morning survived, but some did not.

# MARCH 7, 2005

At six thirty AM a white ibis landed on the front roof, seaweed
in his mouth, and stood still in the tropical rain and wind for
five minutes. His gold, metallic eyes surveying, making plans.
I stood only eight feet from him, my white nightgown almost
transparent in the rain. He lifted himself and flew off through
the small Rauschenberg jungle, past the osprey nest, and gone.
The Florida jungle, calmly repairing itself after the hurricane,
the white morning glories wrapping themselves around the
splintered Australian pines.

# Stained Glass and
# What It Could Mean

At the Catholic church where she doesn't belong she stares at
the stained-glass narratives. She knows all these stories from her
years as a Mormon then a Presbyterian. At another Catholic
church where she doesn't belong there are two girl angels: one
plays the violin, one the mandolin. It is obvious to her gleaming,
secular eyes that these two girls love each other. The beautiful,
sly look of the mandolin angel, feeling the wing of the violin
angel touch her left shoulder. She will never tell where these
two girl angels are, knowing now the violent way some people
she knows would attack these stained-glass girl angels. Violence
and hatred in the name of VALUES. She does not wish to see the
splintered shards of glass, the rainbow of colors in chaos at her
feet. Protecting the stained-glass girls is easy compared to all the
other kinds of protection needed. How much hatred and anger
can the losers withstand from the winners? This is her sum-
mer work, to forgive the winners for their hatred and anger, to
protect the others from the winners. She has been inadequate to
the task.

# VI

# HOCKNEY'S JOYFUL BLUE
# AND PURPLE ROAD

Oh, she wishes he'd never published that book
About measurements and perspectives. Sick
To death of that as a topic of conversation.
Sick of experts with their x-ray machines,
Their MRI machines with canvases and bodies
Lying inside the metallic tubes.
She remembers tears sliding silently
From her closed eyes inside the MRI
Machine fifteen months ago. They'd given
Her space-age goggles that would
Shoot her vision backward through
The end of the tube to a SCENE
From NATURE (the land behind
The clinic's parking lot). But she
Was too afraid to open her eyes.
Ninety minutes of terrible sound
Waves pounding against her
Body inside the silver tube. That day
She decided never to listen to music
Again, then changed
Her mind.

She travels this morning
On Hockney's joyful blue
And purple road. She's cut
This image from so many
Magazines it constitutes
A paper road that could be
Assembled for her to walk on.

Yesterday she cried bitterly
And wrote a long letter,
Amazing heat mingling
With her tears. She
Couldn't figure out
A way to get onto Hockney's
Road. But this morning
She forces herself to embark.
She's no good for anyone
When she's sad. No wonder
She's tried to outlaw sadness
As a way to feel for so many years.

Is it really about being sad? Or about
Being buried by it at times? Isn't her
Sadness about the world trustworthy?
And necessary? If she knew, she might
Have moved off of Botticelli Street
Years ago.

# She Thought, I Am Walking Around My Country

Shirley said, . . . *she thought, I am walking around my country,*
*I am telling its boundaries, describing its edges, enclosing it.*

Whatever mood she's aware of this summer,
She can find the tone of it in one of Jackson's books.
This doesn't seem like particularly good news,
But she is pretty much at peace with Shirley's sorrow.

# Botticelli Street
## and Its Implications

Yes, there's reverence for his genius, the quick nod
Of agreement as long ago the art historian darkened the room
And set the slides spinning. Oh, it's all so old-fashioned
Now—quaint. The young owner of the photography
Store where she drops off her rolls of film tells her
More and more people are trading in their digital
Cameras, and all the dazzling equipment that supports
What she laughingly calls the digital age, returning to their Nikons,

Begging forgiveness. The young owner says Kodak sends more
    and more
Work overseas, though customers always come
Into the store demanding to buy American film.

She remembers how she used to love Fuji Color—
Its metallic green case suited her sense of the future,
The idea of kindly robots with eyes gleaming just
That green.

So there's reverence, right? But Botticelli is not
One of her heroes. And she has so many; how did she
End up living on *his* street? She's back in the room
From so many years ago, with the slides moving up and down
    inside their circle—
She pretends that what she is learning will change
Her life.

And of course, it might have.

# VII

## Describe the Difference between *Depict* and *Evoke*

Botticelli depicted virginal rapture.
Bernini evoked the terror of rape.

If she lived on Bernini Street, she would move.
She knows just enough about his evil deeds to stand
In judgment, though she loves the descriptions
Of his amazing theatrical productions,
His commitment to moving water and
The idea of danger and delight combining
At a safe distance from the audience.

Hockney's road evokes one portrait
Of freedom she can find in the middle
Of the country. She knows the dangers
Of the open road, chooses to abide.

When a beast is hurt it roars in incomprehension.
When a bird is hurt it huddles in its nest.

# Nature Not Culture

Last November on Captiva Island new sea-grape leaves
Formed vertical columns mimicking
Ancient green monuments from Greece
And Rome. They also moved horizontally
To heal the wounded landscape.
My error is understanding both the hurricane
And the leaves. My error leaves me
Unprotected.

# And So It Was I Entered the Broken World

And so it was I entered the broken world
To trace the visionary company of love, its voice
An instant in the wind . . .

Unknown, she too took up the tracing.
Left the broken tower, *saw what the calling was: it was a road I
    traveled, the clear*
*time and these colors of orchards, gold behind gold* . . .

In *Hope*, Muriel was protection;
Today she races ahead with Hart Crane on Hockney's road.

She took up the tracing and discerned
Where love was present, was absent.
She had been programmed for this work
And was full of resentment
For how it wore her down.
Usually the summer heat pounding
On her gave her just enough
Of her version of freedom
To recover, return to her

Tracings. The remarkable heat
This summer couldn't push her
To the other side of her tears,
That blessed cold, vacant place
She used to get to for protection.

And this was her fear:
That the *gold behind gold*
Was this: that she had misunderstood
What she was praying for, that
The path she'd been on
And the prayer without ceasing
Had led to this: all feeling,
All the time.

# TREE OF LIFE MADE BY AN OUTSIDER ARTIST

Therefore photographed in black and white.
Therefore of less value than Cezanne's trees.
Therefore inspiring. Therefore imaginable.
The tree of life made of a million stitches,
The tree of life evoked with thread
And bleeding fingers.
This was of interest to her.
Combine the tree of life
With sewing jackets of nettles
In silence. This made sense
To her, not as performance art,
But as a way to live. Its shocking
Power, its turning away
From humanity. Someone could say,
*Oh, the jackets are for her brothers*
As a way to prove her goodness,
But she would not say it.
Someone might say, *Oh, she doesn't*
*Want her brothers to be swans, to be*
*Ravens*, but how would anyone know
What she wants?

# A Tree Is Not a Human Thing

*A tree is not a human thing, with its feet*
*In the ground and its back hard against the sky;*
*It cannot tolerate the small human tendernesses*
*Moving beneath . . .*

She could see that Shirley Jackson understood.
As one of the guardians, she inspired and oppressed
At the same moment. She became, that summer, another kind
Of hot wind pushing the days forward. ⎯⎯⎯⎯⎯⎯

# VIII

## LOCKED IN WINTER, SUMMER LIES

*Locked in winter, summer lies.*
*Gather your numbed bones under you*
*And rise.*

*Day puts forth its leaves upon night's stalk.*
*Rise,*
*Walk.*

This Barbara Deming poem seems complicated today.
She reads her film studies, falls asleep
Inside Deming's way of combining
Plot explication; psychological theory;
Personal, masked reaction; and the occasional
Film still that matches or does not match
The text. A year ago, she thought Deming
Was speaking directly to her. Today
This may still be true. This lyric moment
Of numbed bones and leaves on the night's
Stalk makes her feel the allegiance deepen.
There's the skeleton being ordered around
(Beseeched?); there's the night stalk

That makes her consider hapless Jack
And his nervous, angry mother, and that cow.
There's the strength of the beanstalk,
And how the leaves became the ladder.
There's the fear, the Giant up in heaven,
Really, and the sense that this is true god
Revealed—carnivorous, desperate to be
Fed, revered, comforted—that god,
With all he's stolen. There's the lyres
Hanging from trees in the Bible
And the golden harp stolen back
And tucked under Jack's arm.
Deming calls it *Variation*
So she knows she's inside a chain
Of sources. Inside, too, her own
Ways of considering. That's
The labyrinth she never quite escapes,
Though nothing is released inside
That labyrinth to assault or destroy her.
She's privileged that way.
She's been taught to see her privilege
That way.

*Locked in winter, summer lies.*

This is completely true.
And this morning she thinks
About the mystery of truth telling.

Tolkien said, *His rage passes description—*
*The sort of rage that is only seen when rich folk*
*That have more than they can enjoy suddenly*

*Lose something that they have long had but*
*Have never before used or wanted.*

So, the Giant as someone with wealth,
So, the Giant as careless, carnivorous god,
So, the Giant as Jack's father.

There's wealth, and hiding, and magic beans.
There's Deming trying to change the world,
Fighting so hard against the aesthetic fog
Some films create—we who watch
Don't understand the fog has rendered us
Invisible, useful to the rich. Deming tried in
Many ways to change the world.
This morning I think of Margaret Hassan
And Barbara Deming, of Jack the thief
And his mother. Do you think his mother
Wanted to be portrayed as she was? No.
One must climb to heaven, steal from god,
To bring a shower of wealth to the little
Mother waiting below. She stares into
Her daughter's beautiful face: Does
The daughter really think she wants
To be perceived in this way, these last
Hot summer days, days she'd imagined
In one way, now utterly wrong and gone?
Can the daughter really think she even
Wants to be seen? To participate?

*Day puts forth its leaves upon night's stalk.*
*Rise,*
*Walk.*

This is the plan for the new day.
She's battled the giant in the clouds
For too long—she chooses instead
Deming's imperative voice, imitating
An intentional genderless Jesus idea.

The white linen unwinds, the skeleton
Never quite gave up on the flesh,
Lazarus and everyone else gets up
And just walks away.

# IX

## *Cutter's Way*: THE WHITE HORSE AND LISA EICHHORN ARE CLEAR

She sobs, helpless, each time she sees the movie, and she sees it
   always
As a shock. Today she'd been not crying, but maybe too tired
   after walking
In blazing heat, and then t'ai chi—always a blessing, but too
   close to a metaphor
For feeling these days—maybe too tired, and surfing through
   channels
And John Heard was there, also blazing, one handed, his pirate
   patch,
His skinny, wounded body, and the amazing Lisa Eichhorn—
   these two
She sees now only on episodes of *Law and Order* (of course they
   amaze
There, too, but not like sinking into *Cutter's Way*, with the war
   coming
Back, backwashed up her gut, her esophagus, and Jeff Bridges
   too pretty,
And the purity of hatred the director felt for the rich. And the
   white horse
That Franz Marc should have painted, but didn't.

47

# X

## THE CHILDREN'S MOON IN THE POEM ABOUT SUMMER

How she used to cringe at her mother's sentimental nature.
How she mirrors it now, cringing at herself. Who cares
About being awakened to see the children's moon?
This is no fairy tale, and her daughter would prefer
To sleep. Truthfully, the daughter would prefer to be
Elsewhere, but she can't quite let her go. No fairy tale
Here, no wicked parents, no dangerous stepparents.
There seems to be a talking cat, but it's just love
He speaks about, not power. He doesn't wear
Dramatic boots, doesn't introduce the daughter
To a life of wealth and pleasure. This summer
The story is about freedom and new paths.
How stupid she was to have missed
The signs.

This morning the children's moon beckoned.
Seriously—it beckoned. A small hummingbird
Moved from flower to flower. The goldfinches
Returned in pairs to sway on the sunflowers.
All of this happened, and its VALUE
Was available, if her soul could just step up.

Sadly, this summer, her soul has had some trouble
Stepping up.

The beauty of the garden was that she hadn't ruined it.
As steward was not found wanting.

For the rest, she needed to recede. She felt herself
As a vanishing point. In the beginning of the summer
She'd been content in the middle distance—had faith
In love and art and the beauty of the night.
Now—diminished by the battle of the Gold Star Mothers,
By the dusty Texas road and the hatred saturating
The air—she was appropriately small. If only
She could shrink like this for the daughter's sake,
Protect the daughter, VALUE the daughter, but
Be very, very small, like the willowy country maiden
From Ryder, or the Indian princess leading her pet deer
Into his imprisoned garden. But less power than either
Of these—not maiden, not princess.

One child called out for the children's moon,
But that was so many years ago.

H.D. cries out, *O, give me burning blue*
*and brittle burnt sea-weed*
*above the tide line,*

*as I stand, still unsatisfied,*
*under the long shadow-on-snow of the pine.*

She had never meant to have any feeling
That would match H.D.'s. You had to have

As beautiful a face as H.D.'s to honor
Dissatisfaction's power.

The one proud to not be a princess left,
Not to enter a forest, not to pine in a tower,
But calmly left for the open space
Of freedom. How easily the mother
Had given her freedom away all those years
Ago. How she felt her daughters battle
Her choices. How mythic,
How boring. The poem itself,
Drenched in Shirley Jackson's sorrow,
Can barely do its work. It's a poem
About summer, so of course it has
More men and women dead in Afghanistan,
More dead in Iraq, more bows to smallness,
To power misused by almost everyone
Including herself.

# XI

## It's a Poem about Summer and Summer Is Over

The Gulf Coast washed out to sea, the dead bodies
Colliding with the oil rigs washed to shore.
New Orleans destroyed, and the National Guard
Who long to help their country instead patrol the dusty
streets and lethal highways of Iraq. It's a poem about summer,
So we thank God that our president had
To cut only two days off his vacation to direct
The vast rescue and rebuilding operation;
It's a poem about summer, so hundreds more
Women and children had to die in honor of
Prayer and holy places and rumors of car bombs.
Some men survive to continue their pilgrimage,
Just some blood—from females, from boys and girls,
From the men pushed down—
Splashed on their feet and calves.
It's a poem about summer, so we safe ones
Feel uneasy about our reverence for benign
Gardens, feel uneasy and rocked by our
Privilege—oh, how we love summer,
How we quote James about the two most
Beautiful words, *summer afternoon, summer*

*Afternoon*, how fortunate we are to know
The words, to read, to feel the end of summer
Wind on our lucky skin.

It's a poem about summer, and Johnny Cash is singing
"Bridge over Troubled Water," and she can hear June's
Voice wavering and powerful, climbing a vine
Between his notes. Once in another life she'd
Walked down the aisle to Paul Simon's *Sail on*
*Silver girl;* now the song tried to comfort
The hundreds of thousands who'd lost everything,
A song about a bridge for a country that seems
To love only the immediate after of calamity and death,
Seems to look only for chances to be on TV loading
Trucks, proving goodness in honor of making it
Onto the evening news. She lives with a man
So humble he won't take credit for all the good
He's done in the actual world, so
The cynic in her is easily alerted by all who
Do not measure up to his stature.
The Flaming Lips were singing now, *And though*
*They were sad they rescued everyone, they lifted*
*Up the sun* and that was the wish
But answered so fast by Tom Waits'
*New corn yellow and          slaughterhouse red*
*The birds keep singing*
*Baby after your dead*
*I'm gonna miss you plenty*
*Big old world*
*With your abalone earrings*
*And your mother of pearl*
So it went on and on.

Her comfort
Was the imagined scene, the good man,
Her husband, driving toward Delaware,
Their youngest daughter beside him,
The two of them singing the entire score
Of *Guys and Dolls* in the plum black midnight.
This would have to do, a slight but worthy protection
In honor of the next day filling with prayer without ceasing,
Not hatred and despair.

Oh, Mason Jennings singing about Paul and Sheila,
Oh, the original painting
That started it all—still tipped against the bookcase,
Resting on the old wooden floor, that path, anonymous
Artist, not Hockney's road, but the possible small
Path to keep walking on—to be steward of the path
And the choice to keep walking.

# Willow Room

That summer Maura and Corey went everywhere
Together. She felt she'd handed over her small
Daughter to some kind of summer enchantress.
She'd get home from work and hear about
Their canoeing expedition, about bike rides
Through city streets in search of the right
Ice cream, about making handmade paper
And staring at the art in the museum so close
To Maura's home. This summer she
Was on strike, never to enter the museum
Until Marc's blue horses were visible, and honored,
But *that* summer she loved the museum
For herself, but mostly for how it gave a world
To Maura and Corey that gleamed with
Promise and beauty. She didn't think
About power much that summer—Maura
The Enchantress had power, she captivated,
And her little daughter followed—
All means of transport used—canoes, kayaks,
Buses, cars, as the two beauties owned the Cities,
From the glass fish to the Lake of the Isles,
From the old-fashioned swing that launched

Them both into summer air, to St. Kate's campus
Where they gathered so many willow boughs
After a storm and carried them back
To her home.

Back from work she heard their voices,
Climbed the stairs, opened the door,
And saw the willow room. Boughs
Wrapped around the canopy, across
All the window frames, hung
From the overhead lights, along
With spinning mobiles handmade
From willow sticks, with bundles of wheat,
Coneflowers, goldenrod, green grass
Turning and turning. Willow room
That smelled wild and free, the outdoors
Brought in, but not really tamed, a far
Thing from tamed. She could barely
Find the girls, and the cat who cared
About love, not power, followed
Her in, stunned and grateful,
And leapt toward the first willow
Branch he saw, indoor cat kept
Inside for love, suddenly
Seeing himself wild, and free.

# GREEN DOOR

Eleven winters ago I saw the green door
For the first time. The tiny cabin
We three traveled to, in honor of sunlight
And heat and friendship. The green door
Drawn, painted, remarked upon, green
Door where I stood before sunrise each
Morning, waiting for light,
Watching cormorant and heron,
Ibis and egret, watching
A summer day begin
In the middle of my own
Winter. Green door a passage
Through, threshold space
To memory and a kind of hope.
The green door gone now
For years, knocked flat
By bulldozers in honor
Of the wealthy, who needed
To flatten five little cabins,
Needed a mansion that could
Hold all the sun, block it
From mere weary travelers.

Green door survives, as do
Some of the birds, the women,
As does the idea of hope.

It's a poem about summer
And summer is over.
Gide said, *In order to discover new lands*
*One must be content to lose sight*
*Of the shore for a very long time.*
The promise was, the poem would end
On her brother Dan's birthday.
And so the poem was ending.
She could feel it slipping through
Her fingers, already aware
Of beloved artists not named,
Aware of how her desire
To not disguise her struggles
Could be seen as false, foolish.

She was a fool for love, though,
And a fool for her children.
She knew the work to become
Transparent; to allow her nerve
Ends to be exposed and available
Was what she had signed up for
This summer. Powerless
She moved forward—pray
Without ceasing, for Brendan's
Knees, for Zach's broken hand,
For every family she knew and didn't know
To be able to keep their children
Safe, for her daughters' powers

And the love in their hearts,
For her husband's goodness,
For everyone she knew in
Transition, from woman to man,
Man to woman,
Lover to alone, child to grown-up,
Soldier to civilian, civilian to soldier,
Immigrant to citizen,
For the son skydiving and the son
Building a hospital, pray without
Ceasing. It's a poem about summer,
And summer is done.

# HOUSEHOLD WOUNDS

# The Drive

The drive toward love
measures itself in the slant of winter
sun breaking on the city left behind,
curving on the bodies of hills.

And the drive toward love is written down
on maps that do not mislead; the map that names
the easiest part: signs, roads, what can be seen.

The car holds its course as I hold mine,
allows no mistakes.
I am the heart inside metal,
the hands that grip the circle,
I am a face in a small mirror,
looking backwards for safety,
looking forward to the "X", the barely decipherable
"me" that lives on the map.

The drive toward love is no myth
though I felt the weight of a story already written,
no new ending requested;
though I felt the row of pines might circle

my car, force me back,
their needles threading the air with the winter word,
intruder.

In the drive toward love nothing is
safe: not the calculated miles of a changeable landscape,
not the words of his voice, "always head north or west",
not the words of passion written down,
memorized like litany,
not even the love traveling the hidden bloodstreams
in all the trails of my body,
all that blood
moving without question,
without hesitation,
toward my heart.

# THE RECLUSE

snapped in two like a brittle pencil
like a fresh bean
she lives in a state
barely useful she does not tamper with herself
left on her own for a few free hours
she does not cause trouble does not bite
does not do anything about
ads she reads are not clipped or filed
whether dealing with new life or new casseroles
she cannot do it     she does not have affairs
does not read
books for a first time always re-reading
old words but she does not memorize
she does not want it that certain

she has never been able to
she does not see people
does not draw conclusions     connections
she cannot do crossword puzzles
she finds things puzzling
veins in leaves     pinecones only at the tops
of certain trees

she loses her purse her mind her baby's pacifier
her tennis shoes in december
her geraniums are dying but
she knows the image has been used before
some hot-house poet always beating her
to the punch

she reads campaign literature that arrives
secretly under her locked door
she casts a vote and lost thinking suddenly of
the privilege of a secret ballot she cannot remember
how to open the curtain     she thinks of buying a voting booth
and making her home inside except she knows
it will be misrepresented     misread
too mystifying

she knows it is november
she feels certain some planet is blocking her
claustrophobic she chooses to rest in small rooms
anyway
big rooms demand so much
filling

# Pursuit

After she is lured from safety the scene begins.
We do not see what has enticed her, why she wants
it enough to risk the slow movement from the dark
into broken patterns of sunlight on the forest floor.

Fur settled on her skin, eyes without panic,
no sign of a heartbeat out of control.
A normal wild scene; these trees, this sunlight,
roots, weeds, other creatures, the stream.

And she is a part of all this. Not one of us
who sees her can remember we have never seen
her. Now she begins to run; this too looks
right. She, lithe, smooth to touch,

bright eyes running, looks right running
and no one wants to stop her. No.
So she runs. The scene, suddenly ominous, certain
trees too large and sparse, undergrowth tangled,

a harsher green. The stream distended,
over-running its banks. She runs faster now,
pursued by what we cannot see, cannot guess.
We have watched her too long now,

and harmless, easy on the eyes, she compels
our attention; we care how her story ends.
She cares too, and with no break in her stride
she races out of sight, into a darker

region of the forest where our eyes cannot focus,
cannot find her, where our feet do not take us.
And because there is only so much we can give, we turn
our care for her into metaphor, and gracelessly walk away.

# The Man Who Knew
## about Winter

He wondered why she moved through the house singing over
and over, "so long, it's been good to know ya." And he won-
dered why all the poems and stories he'd been collecting for
years were disappearing from his notebooks; every time he
opened one there were more clean, white pages, more indenta-
tions left from paperclips that had done something useful, more
erased chapter headings.

He wondered why he knew so many women for the first time
in his life, why they were all beautiful, slim like weasels, slim
like the fantasy woman he kept hidden in his brain, and why
the woman who was right this minute walking past him sing-
ing, "so long, it's been good to know ya," was, although quite
good looking, solid, tall, certainly not the kind of woman to
tremble, reed-like, in a winter storm, was more likely to grab a
snow shovel and do the right thing with it. Well, it was winter,
and he supposed everything needed a second look, deserved a
second or third look, he guessed that was why he was suddenly
so introspective, so consumed with doubt; his notebooks, his
woman, fed up with women, bugged by the kids, he guessed
that winter was why but that made no sense, winter, after all,
was his favorite season. Only a month ago he'd sworn never

to move; he was going to dig in, he'd told a friend, he was no
weakling, he was no sun worshipper, hell, no.

So he listened to this woman in the kitchen singing her old
cowpoke song, wondered if she was imagining tumbleweeds,
cactus, was seeing lizards move across secret sand, what was she
doing? The food was cooking, the children were gone, popular
children, invited here and there, sometimes he wondered how
she kept it all straight, how in the middle of her song, on any day,
she would call out, "It's four-thirty, time to pick up Joe or pick up
Sally," or time to do something else so that something else could
happen later on, in time. Time after time she surprised him, mov-
ing as she did, chanting poems, recipes, songs, phone numbers;
he remembered she'd told him once her memory was lousy, but
she was a liar. Her memory was frightening.

He wondered why he was happy with all this confusion,
with a woman singing in the bedroom, "so long, it's been good
to know ya," the sounds of drawers being opened and closed.
When he fell asleep he wondered why the woman felt suddenly
slim like a weasel, slim like fantasy brides, why she hummed
in her sleep, why she was suddenly all the women he knew so
well, why spring didn't come sooner, why days ended with such
grace, why all his nights were like wrapped presents: dreams, the
woman, restful sleep.

He supposed winter did this to him. When he woke up he
saw that his notebooks were filled again, there were new chap-
ter headings, written in brown ink, when he woke up the chil-
dren were home, he remembered their faces as if they had never
been gone, he heard the woman singing in the kitchen, a quiet
song, but it did not sound like a trail song, did not sound like
a going away song, did not sound like a blues song, it sounded
correct, like the voice of a woman he used to know, supposed
he still knew, sounded like a woman who sang haunted rock

and roll songs, who paced the house with an imaginary micro-
phone in her hand. He decided to give her a real microphone
for Christmas, for Chanukah. It was still winter, he knew
December was real, he knew he made her happy. He didn't
understand why, but she kept on not leaving, and that was
good enough for him.

# THIS AFTERNOON

is like another and another and that is
no simile I don't even like this afternoon
but a poem waits to be written
there's the smell of dinner cooking a voice
singing tub water running small daughter
calling orders from her world of water
and the man who sits patiently
cataloguing a life he lived without me
each slide holds this memory or that memory
click and he keeps them organized keeps them
dust free keeps them alive with each
click keeps them coming in order click
this perfect pine tree this perfect sun
set this perfect woman click this life
he left behind to sit with me this poet
woman with dinner cooking and a small
girl bathing and the stereo sending the
message of lost love this woman sitting in a
winter afternoon writing a poem click
about a man click who has so many pictures
from his past whose past is so clear framed
preserved protected the past that won't

stay in the past because he clicks it into
the present tense the past that hovers
the past that becomes the present as he
walks out at four-thirty on this afternoon
to go see the perfect woman who is always
present from his past the perfect woman
click who is not me.

# Extended Metaphors

They are my present triumvirate.
They speak: she is the sun,
no, the moon,
no,
a star.

They forget me as they battle to define
me. All three pretend to hate war,
all carry their wounds differently, enjoy
presenting their scars; the stitches of their various
doctors give them pleasure. I can see none of them
as astronauts; too bad,
since I am placed in the sky.
At the moment they are brand-new lawyers, over-eager, filled
with facts, their texts more precious than anything
my earthly hands might give.

Sun: I am unhurried, daytime steady, constant,
I burn out so slowly he doesn't worry about losing
me. I last, grant new life,
am not selective when I give warmth.

Moon: I control tides, I am the secret,
I am cyclical, I am rose blood monthly, I should be
dark haired but he forgives me, blonde will do for now,
I am the cause of tidal waves, beautiful in my coming,
awesome then forgotten
in the terrible rebuilding of his landscape.
I disappear, slipper small, luminous only in memory,
I haunt, bear mysteries, not children.

Star: I am some light. I do not fit
into constellations already plotted,
I burn only myself, I light emptiness pointlessly,
I am already gone when he sees my shining,
I plummet, fall endlessly,
my long descent delights him.

He says, "Oh look, a falling star."
and kisses his new lover,
while I do my meteoric dive,
while I am dying,
all the while hoping I break
open, burn out, turn to hard, black rock
inside ocean.
I do not want to die on land.

What they have done to me
no longer is a question worth answering.
I know I can no longer bear
being personified by any
one but myself.

I am the tree, no, not that one,
I am here, smaller than any star,
I am rooted, though I understand why I forget
that truth sometimes; I travel long distances
for lost water sources.

In the winter I am so filled with death
even I forget I live.

I have not been done in by some reckless bonsai gardener.
I am not an easy species.

I cause no natural disasters
except my own.

Next year, after I receive spring's fair gift,
I plan to become a woman.
We'll all see what will come of that
metaphor.

# THE SORCERESS

*I*

The sorceress returns from another hard day,
too tired to clean the castle,
practice her mail-order chants, mix potions,
change anyone's life for the better.

She needs her eight hours.
Since her return from the sea she has not dreamed.

The tape recorder attached to her telephone
is always filled with sobbing voices.
Mothers-in-law, randy, straying husbands,
children gone bad,
the petty needs of the people wear her to a frazzle.

She has never learned to say no with any authority.
Her successes are legendary, but her castle is a mess.

## II

Her jester's toes have forgotten how to dance.
His bells are rusting.
He cannot juggle anymore.
He sits in the kitchen, trying to recover
his lost art, but the apples roll on the floor.
The cook is fed up. She wants only a floor safe to walk on.

The jester believes he can no longer amuse the sorceress.
His mother's words haunt him,
"Yes, but can you make a living at it?"

## III

The sorceress walks through town.
Children, no longer crippled, play kick-the-can.
They do not recognize her.
Grateful mothers trail her,
pressing fresh vegetables into her hands.
The sorceress tries to decline.
She has no appetite.

The sorceress retreats into the forest, carrying her burdens.
No one follows.
The villagers believe the forest is where she does
her best work.
It is not.
She goes there only to gather wildflowers.
She presses them between sheets of waxed paper
during sleepless nights.

## IV

A red-haired sailor is waiting for her
when she returns from the woods.
He tries to crowd her.
She cannot believe he has misunderstood.
Has he never heard of shipboard romances?

He believes in his charm.
He believes his body has cast an unbreakable spell on hers.

She knocks him into the moat, crosses over,
orders the guards to lift the drawbridge.
She assumes he can swim.

## V

The sight of the sailor has helped.
This night, like a doctor unwilling
to be on call, she unplugs her phone.

She uses her gift,
creating a wine to drink for dreaming.
She goes to sleep knowing
her night will be rich with tangled plots,
unsought images, the colors of the sea,
the boat, lost in fog.

In her body's final turning before dawn,
the face, luminous, of her loss,
hovers behind her closed eyelids.

When she wakes, her heartbeat has slowed
to a more human rate.

She rings for breakfast.
The cook's eyes fill.
"I believe the crisis has passed once more.
If she asks to see the children,
things may get back to normal around here."

V I

Music fills every turret.
The jester opens up the main ballroom and begins
brushing up on his tap dancing.
The sorceress and her children are laughing
in the nursery.
The phone rings incessantly.
The callers cannot contain themselves,
begin to speak before the beep.

V I I

The sorceress knows the fever has passed.
Her hands are not shaking, her children's eyes
neither give nor reflect any unhealthy sorrow.

She has known for years that surviving
is her greatest talent.
The rest has always flowed
from the acquired magic.

# THE WOMAN WHO KNEW
## ABOUT WINTER

Times her heart beat normally, brain waves scanned to the rhythm of a waltz, ah, Vienna, those times more than others she knew winter was the reason, the cause, the answer, the question.

True, sometimes she thought winter was only the cause, usu-ally she knew better, but now that the snow was sifting through the windows, now that the cats had left town, their knowledge of migration patterns a mystery and misery to her bird-loving friends, now she wondered.

Her children polished their skate blades, sang winter songs on key, her daughter particularly caught by the phrase, "Three turtle ducks and a park in a pear tree," her son particularly caught by his sister's ignorance of song lyrics. They were busy, had their own lives already and the oldest was only six. So, she would wander away from their lyrical disagreements, leave them in the echo of their words, a last refrain of "Santa Claus is com-ing to town" ringing in her ears. She would go to her bedroom, haven from the real world; sometimes the woman worried about calling her bedroom a haven, worried about the implications, what did she think constituted the real world, anyway? She could remember with very little effort the loving, the gentle words, certain details of the man's hands, she knew those things were part of the real world, so why did she, when alone, hesitate, call those things, by implication, an illusion?

There was no answer. Or: there was an answer, no doubt hidden inside rock and roll lyrics, but lately she had been unable to turn the channel selector away from the classical station. And what did that mean, she asked, having gotten out from under the last question. What did it mean to suddenly be choosing to play music with no words? She was not a snob; even though she played classical music she always referred to it as music with no words, as if the words were the things to be valued. She didn't want anyone thinking she knew the names of concertos, knew any of the numbers or flats or sharps that composers assigned to their noted genius. She knew *The Pastoral Symphony* and *The Mouldau*, the latter because her college roommate was a Smetana junkie, had to listen to *The Mouldau* once a day or she couldn't deal with the pressure of undergraduate life. The point was that whenever the woman heard classical music she liked, if she was with someone else, she always asked, "Isn't that *The Pastoral Symphony?* No, I mean, *The Mouldau?*" and of course it wasn't either of them, though she had honestly thought it could have been.

She supposed that those two memorized titles indicated that she wanted secretly to live in the country by a river. But that couldn't be since she not secretly at all wanted to live by the Atlantic Ocean near a city with forty movie theaters, in a climate without snow, but which possessed bracing winds, occasional stunning storms, and well, perhaps snow that fell once in ten years, or once in a hundred, as it did in Florence and Rome.

The woman realized in the time it had taken to explain this much she had arrived back to the idea of winter, back to the actual word snow. No, actually, since this was no word game, back to the actual snow that was no longer sifting but was instead piling up in her room.

And, although the woman generally loved to think about what was hidden inside, or buried underneath other things, snow held out no mystery worth solving. It was what it was, and what it was she wanted no more of. She was no regional writer, afraid of permanent writer's block if she changed landscapes. She knew more poems and stories were hiding everywhere: in the everglades, in the jungles, in the empty deserts, were waiting in every town she'd never seen, in every place she'd never walked.

And she came to see that winter was not the cause, or effect, was not the answer or the question. Was not even a symbol since symbols are rarely so cold, rarely turn to slush, rarely invade whole rooms with their real presence. The point was: what could she do with it now that she had it? And, she knew all too well, what she could do with it was live with it or leave. And why she didn't leave was the chapter that was hiding inside the typewriter keys. Unfortunately, the room where she wrote was adrift with sifting piling snow, and the typewriter was buried and the spring thaw was nowhere in sight, although signs of rebirth were everywhere.

She knew enough to seek warmth, but she was not a bird, migration was not a natural talent, and since she hated birds anyway she hadn't used a bird metaphor for years. She was not planning to fly away, just to leave gracefully like a human whose heart beats in three-quarter time should do, when they finally admit winter is no longer their natural element.

# What Will Last

To say what hurts:
all the why's spread out like cold
butter, wrecking the last piece of bread
in the house.

Who's to say what words
will soothe
if you could only feel them pierce
your mind, precise, painless
arrows.

Who's to say how long
we might last:
longer than the time before at least,
as if we thought we could apply
for any warranty longer than seven years.

Who's to say except you and me;
we rise and fall in this house,
our bodies huddled over jigsaw puzzles.
I lose my sense of what piece fits where,
trying to stop every ordinary activity
from turning relentlessly
into a puzzle I cannot solve.

We rise and fall,
our bodies meet and are put back together,
we are the jigsaw puzzle that works,
fits at least one more time.

Who's to say we might not
survive our own disparate yearnings
each time they emerge.

We face off against our own shadows
longing for high noon
when we can forget
for a moment
that they exist.

# THE MOTHER

*For Virginia Wells Bowman*

your meeting at yellowstone
the mountains were a fact
you did not realize they could be lost through love
so you traveled to him across plains       east
mormon woman       what travesty to head for daybreak's edge
aiming your heart like an arrow at that gray-eyed
presbyterian

home home you said to yourself
the lush flat green of prairie
when did your eyes begin to ache for the rockies
perhaps when he said the names
nakomis       johanna       minnetonka
the lakes of this northern state
no fair exchange for your loss

but did we not play pioneer so adequately
for his gray eyes
dressed in aprons stained with the juice of currants
wild raspberries
we filled the fruit cellar with proof
of love       adaptability

the years of harvest passed
he fell ill      grew oblivious
to your slow rooting
in the flat lands where passion led you

and you grew only stronger
your now midwestern hands are still
holding back the wilderness
and shaping inner forms of children's children

like the mountains you left
you are strong      steady
you endure      like they      the terrible winds
the change of season
you endure time's unceasing movement
through all your landscapes

# THE FATHER

*For Clifford A. Bowman*

three acres
pale moon garden that was my father
lilacs carried in burlap from pennsylvania
for his new home
pine trees planted      now old and scarred
brush fires set by careless children

rosebushes tethered to spikes of oak or birch
the flowers he eased through
late spring snows      grasping grape vines
planted too near
evenings he watched the vines lean and bent them new

this garden      now run and staked by strangers
where my summers passed endless
hoe and rake      my fingers watching his
"you must learn to press the seeds into earth this way"

the horizontal maple
stripped of branches for firewood
the trunk left whole for my sake
barked pony of childhood wishes

now flowerless suckers tear my hands
I do not coax rosebuds from this over-run plot
the grapevine tangles and gives no fruit

only the lilacs endure these winters
this neglect
there are fewer sprigs each spring
no one has ridden my maple horse
and moss and insects rejoice
in their hollowed paradise

# HOUSEHOLD WOUNDS

You are cutting apples for your children.
You are committed to their health, and with every bite
they swallow your guilt is appeased,
somewhat, the guilt you feel buying bubble gum,
or the guilt you feel handing out cookies at 4:30,
when you know real food, a proper dinner
will march out of the oven at 5:00.
A digression: you are still cutting
apples, and the knife searches for a truer direction,
and your second finger meets the blade
and red apple blood runs
down the drain.

You are reading bedtime stories. An important
ritual, such a right thing to do
it amazes you. Nights your children would rather
play one more game of octopus eating a submarine
you lose your temper, say sternly, books
or bed, that's your option. You can't help it;
you believe in books, and tonight, reading
*Leo the Late Bloomer*, you are so happy,
the children lean into your body, their elbows

find spaces of you never before explored,
you reach to turn the page and
your son says, don't cry
as he watches you cry,
a paper cut that sliced
open your third finger,
page five,
more blood.

You are learning to be handy. You want
to build bookcases, repair the furnace, chop
wood and celery, you want to do it
all, and you want to do it all
right. Your therapist warns you
every week, you can't do it
all. Well, you know that. You hold up
your hands in surrender; the smashed thumb
awarded by the hammer, the airplane you built your son
has flown away, your thumb reminds you
of your accomplishment.
The two fingers wrapped in band-aid sheer strips,
the angry burn that hides in your palm,
you touch it and remember cooking your first
batch of spaghetti, you touch it
and remember how you forgot
to use hot pan holders.

No one can see the symmetrical line of bruises
that linger on your left leg; you, falling off steps,
you, shovelling the snow that won't stop
falling, just like you won't stop
falling.

The headache from standing up under the stairwell,
you always forget to remember the potential for harm
in a home; you don't want paranoia
to rule you.

You want: the walls smooth, the steps untreacherous,
you want the ceiling to stay up, the lightbulbs lit,
the linoleum flat, the rugs glued in place,
the toys put away, the cutlery dull, the scissors
hidden, the needles and pins melted down and used
for some vital part of an airplane that will take you
away from all this
danger.

# MENDING

just to match thread and fabric
takes a year

a needle sharp enough
an eye big enough to pass through
to see clearly from
exactly what it is that needs mending

just to match the torn place
with a patch
that will not call attention to itself
takes more than years

just to find what's been torn
and what's worth mending
seems like years go by

and my hands are not graceful
or kind about this task
they dial my mother's number
they speak with my voice over the wires
mother they say will you mend this
will you mend this too

and though she agrees
as I knew she would
there's so much mending to be done
and what has been torn
will take years to mend
and I cannot ask her for that much
time

it's my turn to mend
and I won't tell anyone
how long it might take

# After

### I

you've seen a three foot long
white cat watching you from a fence
in Scotland there's not much left.
No one believes you anyway;
you put amazement away in a junk drawer
of feelings you no longer harbor.

### II

After you've had the babies,
have screamed with the slash of new life,
well, then, all the pain your men feel
with their cut fingers, aching stomachs,
spring colds, it leaves you cold.
No sympathy, ice heart, you don't care.
Want to scream: get off your back,
go to work, you don't know, you don't know.
They call that narcissism.
Women I know well suffer that dread disease.

### III

After you've lost your best friend
to an insatiable cancer that consumed her,

well then, other conversations seem
inconsequential. No energy for small talk,
big talk. She's just dead. Burned to ash
wearing the pink nightgown you gave her;
you don't bother going to the grave,
she's not there anyway, still inside
putting pressure on your heart, appearing
in alternate frames of a Japanese movie,
hiding in the way some women have of holding
china teacups.
Stopping you in the middle of love-making,
slight smile: do it for both of us she says.

## IV

After you're not so young anymore.
Too much behind you to feel new, not much
to do with the dizzy feeling of being
your own stranger in a place you name home
for lack of more accurate words. After you
pace and play Salt Lake solitaire until your
hands bleed with the shuffle, after you throw
all the photo albums out the window, after all
this you find out it's only ten in the morning
and the sun is leaving again, just like always.

## V

After all this time you can't quite figure out what keeps you
here besides the kids, the poem, the smell of lilac invading
your room, as your friend without wings does a slow dive
outside your window and you can't even catch the hand she
offers you in her grace-filled descent. After all this time.

# WHAT IT IS

springs from this deep hollow
like the space air fills
under the bird's arcing motion.

This emptied feeling,
china cup that will never be filled.

Spring air and I falter
in the blue, in the warm,
this sound that can find

no voice in free air.
Deep hollow echoes nothing
but loss, loss, I want

to frame it,
I want to cage it,
walls of blood,

luminous it should shine
to disturb the dark
with the message of emptiness.

Dark stone descending,
endless fall,
well with one wish left;

I am leaving
this age, I am leaving
the children whose birthdays I celebrate.

Where the sound of new life disappears,
that's where I go,

dark hollow I join you.
We will grow
again together,

deep blood, smooth stone,
married we emerge in a colder time.

Must I take care of you
this whole lifetime left?
What is cherished here?

# The Subject

*In Memory of Wendy Parrish*
*Dear Friend 1950—1977*

### I

We will paint this picture now,
the only one worth painting, at once
compelling, inviting,
an essential background, blue sky,
sun, of course, heat should shimmer
off the canvas.
We are doing well, novices no longer,
add some trees, for shade, for beauty,
then the water, moved by imperceptible wind,
this is our canvas, not mine alone,
so the wind must be controlled.

The canvas has been stretched, now must stretch more
to include brown and gold children.
The child with daylight hair, the child
whose hair carries the reminder of autumn.
These children are moving
on the canvas, they move for too many reasons
to list, just let them move, on or off
the canvas; they help carry the picture's
true message.

Off to one side the mother rests, her face turned
to sun; let it be seen in this painting
that she is willing it all to continue.
Let it be understood: she can be motionless
because the other guards
these painted children.
The mother's face should be at once fierce and peaceful.
A hard face to capture.

The canvas expands, we artists cannot stop
the images we collect, the canvas
can bear all these scenes, collected in so many
pairs of eyes, the canvas wants to contain
all that is remembered.

## II

The central figure in this painting
is moving at the water's edge
in lilac, in navy blue, and the temptation
is strong in me, I want to add the wind
that will move her hair, that will push her scowling
back to me, saying, "Hell, this wind. I don't know why
you enjoy it so much."
I want my answer included on the canvas. "Look,
we share this disagreement, and few others. Go ahead,
call the children, then help me
pack up this clutter, all right, call the children.
We will go home. The wind in the city will be kinder."

## III

The canvas will not dry. God knows I have placed
it in cool rooms, hot rooms, have placed it against
trees in winter wind, in spring sun, but the paint

will not dry, it shines, the canvas is not full,
wants more,
we artists have worked hard, and although we have succeeded
in some ways,
      that background,
      the children,
      these women,
there is so much more the canvas
hungers for, and there is not one among us
who would not have chosen, give the chance,
to have image after vision after image
collect, always there would have been
too much to paint, so much we would have put
our brushes down with relief, let ourselves
fall into this constantly incomplete canvas.

IV

We will paint this picture now,
the only one worth painting.
No gallery can deny us as we move relentlessly
into another summer.
      The sun,
      the children,
      the mother,
alone now, alert to their every motion.
She will not turn her face to the sun as often
this season,

and on some other canvas her face will be
shadowed, eyes liquid,
some essential sorrow painted there
that no brush strokes away.

# A Poem about White Flowers

my father chose a train
gave it the gift of his body
bright july sun
the engine lifted his form
hurled it      scattered it      moved on
we pretended there was enough left
to cremate

and the white flowers you gave me are so right
they fill my home      I think of them
slashes of petal white
I play endless game after endless loss
of solitaire
just so I can sit with those slashing white flowers
I love these flowers from you
they surprise me the way the roses didn't
they touch me the way a good white cliché
is supposed to touch all women who believe
in words like white and fragrance      who believe
in daisies pretending to be zinnias and in daisies
swearing they are white chrysanthemums

by the tracks my brother searched
for father's property
july sun burning to nothing the last
fragments of my father's beautiful
piano hands
he found the wallet       torn pictures
pieces of identity that identified
a man who came to dread his own

by the train station my brother found
two lovers who had been giving each other
their bodies
when they heard the train's emergency scream
they forgot the pleasure they had been seeking
and sought another
when they looked up the air carried
my father toward them       they were frightened
by the blood       the choice of death
so near their open fields of love

and the white flowers you gave me
don't fade today       the white
phosphorescent against a winter gray window
I love them for not fading today
for being white       not red       not dying       not red
for being white and themselves
whatever they are       whatever they become

# July Twenty-Seventh,
# Nineteen Seventy-Nine

### I

My father's death certificate looks casual.
Some hand on this date eight years ago wrote:
"Direct cause: mangling. Engineer applied brakes.
All reasonable effort made to avoid contact." Well,
there you have it.

### II

When my brother wrote me the letter he said,
"There was nothing left but little pieces."
I cried again, though living in Denmark only one
other person could hear me and he is gone too,
less violently, the loss as incalculable.

### III

The death certificate is white. The print dark blue.
This morning I sat in my usual chair,
my mother talking to me of wills, insurance,
money, the house, talking about facts.

It rained all night, that slow steady kind
that doesn't scare.
As we sat talking the blue, deep blue sky broke
through the gray, like his eyes, my most easily traced
legacy from him.

## IV

I keep hidden other gifts passed along.
Inside this eight year old scar I carry the imprint
of bad weather and of a single hot July morning.
That's me: married to heat and bad weather.
Inside the heart I carry serious truths
about ways to die, about ways the cards are dealt,
about the way life goes wrong.
Inside my mind are his poems, written with a pseudonym,
though he was not ashamed of his name or words.

## V

Father. I write all my poems with my true name.
Father. I write all my poems so I may bury you more kindly.
Father. I write all my poems to keep you alive.
Father. Your gravestone is too small, horizontal with the earth.

That's not good enough. I will dig it out.
I want the headstone vertical, parallel with trees,
hollyhocks, parallel with my stance as I stare down
at where your small pieces, burned and burned, hide.
I want things parallel now, poem for poem,
gray eyes to gray eyes,
track to track.

# How I Will Know
# When the War Is Over

we are all assigned wars
we are all assigned friends who die
in war     during years of private war
we are all assigned men to love who burn
draft cards     go to prison
we are all assigned men who conscientiously object
to everything
but peace

I thought my war was over
all my patient marching
my strong left hand writing slogans on flags
to carry on my strong left shoulder

I thought my war was over
when my friend with one leg blown away
in war blew his brains out carefully in his garage
his strong right hand holding the gun

I thought my war was over
when I stopped writing poems
about nixon and god and babies burning

I was wrong
today all this week all last week
the war comes back
I was wrong because my son says
"today I met a man who writes about vietnam.
was that your war, mom?"
I was wrong because my son says
"here's a picture in the paper of that man.
does he say the words of war in his story?"
I answer and realize my son wants to share my war
until he gets one
of his own

we are all assigned children to love
they may not come from our bodies      that hardly matters
but we all must claim children to love
we are all assigned children to learn from
to teach the wearying truths of war to

we are all assigned a war and I have mine
I must not forget
that the title of this poem is a lie
there will never be any way for me to know
that the war is over

# ONE ANGEL THEN

# ANGEL FISH NEW LIFE

When I am most able to leave my lungs behind,
when I am most free of the form I hide inside,
when water is not the only home worth having,

then I'll ascend, from darkness of sea earth,
or rise from the muted excuse for soil deep
in ocean beds.

Then I'll rise, fish-winged and halo-ed,
smooth, with eyes that will never close again,
I'll rise like all angels, so pure and good,
move through fathoms of air, new air,
learn to breathe in, breathe out, like angels
should, learn to move my wings, like angels
must.

I'll rise from the blue green, colorless
world, and seaweed won't lace me in, won't
tangle my smooth scales which will rise
with me, angel, leader of forgotten fish,

rise from a water home, hurry through the skies,
swim through atmospheres alien and natural.

I will be that rising fish woman, angel, angel
they'll call me, angel in water and sky,
armless, winged, with eyes that won't close,

angel fish swimming through heaven where gods
have no arms, no wings, angel fish swimming
through air, no reward for all that change
except holiness.

# Living with Angels

my children are cold
angels in the snow.

the angels stay behind
when i call my children in.

the cold white angels
in reverse relief

float over the hillsides,
no more children inside.

these angels lift
from hills, winter angels,
and there is nowhere to get warm
when you are holy and white.

most people think
and their thoughts are mud,
or slip through bleachers,
most people think and the air
goes crazy with bad energy.

avoid crowds: there's so little
protection, and minimal rewards
for mixing,

but when jesus thought something big,
the form of his thoughts became an angel.
he couldn't help it. even when he thought,
"where's my sandal?" an angel, small and quiet,
came to the world.

when jesus thought large things like parables,
and especially when he changed little food
to much, and when he drove the money changers
from the temple, those times angels filled
the air, clouds of angels encircled him,
some wanted to carry him away, he was so
heavenly, they sighed, but he was tied
to earth, while his thoughts grew wings.

there were times jesus grew weary
of the endless transformations,

even what he dreamed, alone, under stars,
changed into angels more beautiful than he,

dressed more cleanly, possessing wings
to lift them from the hot sand, away
from what he had to stay for.


jesus was at once confounded and jealous
of these angels; they were made from his mind


yet lived apart, evanescent, joy-riding
as he shared his time with weary lepers,
anxious disciples.


his thought forms made the air dense
with angel traffic and sometimes in his slow
progression through towns the air was so
heavy with wings he could hardly breathe.


the clutter in the sky grew immense, but
only he could see them, he parted angel
wings with his hands, just to walk, when
he woke in the morning new angels hovered
where his dreams were born.


these were warm angels, born near desert,
who have never met the cold angels left
behind by children.


only children who cannot obey the call
in winter turn to angels themselves,
frozen in red snowsuits, relief on hills,
they become angels under soil,
buried deep and sleeping,
wings trying to move the earth.

when we rest on white sheets i press my arms
in a wing pattern and your arms move to match
them.
we are one angel then, a warm angel with
wings inside shared skin; no swan can match
us, no god in disguise disturb us.

we take the shape of this angel, carry it
into worlds where we move alone; this is
a quiet angel, rarely challenged, who emerges
again when time connects us.

this angel lives in two,
like the child inside the angel on the hill,
like each separate angel inside jesus,
born one by one.

the world is an invisible angel place.
when our eyes see something we can't believe,
when our hands touch something insubstantial,
when we hear the feathered hush in dreams,

those are angels attending us,
heavy with wings and silence,
who wait for us to rise and join them.

discouraged by our humanness,
our knife-bright desires
that tie us to the earth.

"... *they are preserved from change and consequently
do not fall within the order of time* ..."

E. GILSON, *The Christian Philosophy of St. Augustine*

the saint speaks of angels here,
excluding me before i have time
to draw my next, human breath.

times i have preserved myself from change
i have been like a fallen angel, blood
on my skin and driven by time.

when change became the way to live
i wanted to move like angels move
through lives, leaving singular blessings.

but, unable to stay because time pressed
me on, the blessings grew perverse,
there was a darkness in eyes i loved.

my arrivals and departures only emphasize
my humanness. i run but do not fly,
afraid of certain changes, afraid to be

caught before i know if i have changed enough,
have run away for the last time.
i do fall within the order of time, the language

time speaks is my native tongue.
i measure my life not with moments but in
hours, i preserve myself from making a choice

as time moves like a dark angel
through my life, changing me slightly
with each dip of winged night or

broken day. the angel in me grows
smaller, smaller,
diminishing my claims for holiness,

turns smaller, grows tired, wings beating
inside my human heart, unable to choose
another life, so small and lost inside mine.

# SPACE ANGELS

*The angels may land downtown.*

JACQUES VALLEE, *Invisible College*

Joseph Smith met his angel in the woods
three times. His angel was clean, had
a name, wore white; in his first disguise
he came as a "pillar of light."

Often, angels dressed in sunlight touch down
in forests, or in wide, white space of deserts,
often, angels visit those we don't trust, then
we wonder about them, who they are in league
with, how they choose whom they choose
to speak to.

I wonder that, the dreamers who desire a
spaceship to carry them away say that "angel"
is just another word for an unidentified flying
object. god weeps; how many angels have drifted
down to earth, been mistaken for martians,
their raiment labeled spacesuit, their halos
called helmets.

The angel brought the golden plates to Joseph
Smith. He sat behind a dark curtain, translating
the myths though just a farm boy, unskilled at
foreign tongues. And who could believe that?

Enough did.

Fatima claimed she was visited by god in the
form of angels. Fatima fell in a cold faint,
blood pressure dropping, dark face lightening.
Fatima was visited by ones from another world
and the science shining from the spaceship
dropped her to the ground, their reversed,
spiraling isomers, left-spiraling as if from the
devil, turned her pale, left her a legend.

All the visitations, the holy moments stolen
alone leave the human scarred, eyes aglow
with trance and mystery. We are afraid of them,
for them. We turn away, we follow.

Modern, we long for ancient rites and surprise.
When the foreign ones flame into the deeps,
set up home, we linger in the ocean, wanting
to be drawn down to a new world, we want all
the light inside the ocean to be candles
lit against the darkness in our lives.
Sometimes any visit counts; we would gladly
turn pale, speak in languages not our own,
let pillars of light blind us with radiance.
We think we would risk that dislocation
from our own lives. I think I would risk

that dislocation from my life. When the angels
land downtown I want my arms extended
in welcome, my eyes ready for blinding
mystery,
my skin ready for an angel's touch.

# THE EYES TO SEE ANGELS

*Open is broken. There is no breakthrough without*
*   breakage. A struggle with an angel, which*
*   leaves us scarred, or lamed.*

                        NORMAN BROWN, *Love's Body*

*I*

Maybe it's as simple as this: the eyes to see
angels are not born into all, there's no hereditary
design, no parents in quiet mating can make eyes

like that. Sometimes you come on angels because
snow's white, and beckons, or because Mary's
acquiescence never seemed more logical than
when your eyes looked at the wild-winged man
angel who brought the news. The pull of the
ocean, the phosphorescence streaking under the
skin of the sea, that light is not of the earth,
other-worldly, you say to yourself, on a cape
night when nothing is good enough for you
but angels.

They suddenly appeared, in any form your mind
allowed you to conjure. The need for angels,
their diaphanous presence, doesn't just ignite
Fatima, or saints done in by hard times,
but pulls you too, your hand burning with
the touch of a dead woman's skin, soft angel hair.


## II


I wanted to say to a friend: just let them come
in, but I'm not that easy either, my friends need
sleep, so do I sometimes; I send the angels
spinning in orbits away from me, so weary
of their gifts.

Alberti said: "The world, being the world, fits
in a child's hand." I know that, know there's
so little time that it's hard to follow such
ephemeral flights. The times hurt, and I have
found some broken angels, wings intact, with no
desire to rise, and I have found people who want
an angel's protection but not their sudden,
capricious flight. Why angels? Because there's
ocean, and unexplained light, and so much
darkness to live in anyway, because there's
a man who led me to angels. Because I see
how angels are caught too, their longing
for holiness, and the fiercer desires that
confound them, and though they linger in time,
held still by a reckless god, their eyes
are too human to run from.

Their hearts pump a winged fever of wanting,
and even when I turn away they wait, want to
live through me, though I am earthbound,
rarely incandescent. Their secret ways
and easy entrances break my days and nights,
mark me indelibly, human face scarred, eyes
burnt by what they make me see.

# THE ONLY WINDOW THAT COUNTS

# What My Daughter Asked about the Angel in the Tree

There's a mountain ash on fire outside the only window
that counts, and the children grow restless seeing
autumn is the end of things.

Why don't we let the angel of the tree inside?
We've got no money to leave home with,
and the architecture of our rooms spares us beauty
and little else.

Oh, let that angel in. This is no annunciation;
his wings are on fire, his sorrow is audible,
and we are cold enough to be useful,
lonely enough to be warmed.

# Formal Presentations of Love

### I

The exchange of letters.

### II

The exchange of silence, which causes no fear, which we take
for solace, which we take as a sign of a match, not one which
kindles a small flame, to light a cigarette, or to purify a needle,
signifies a match, which means it is easy to be silent together,
which implies a closeness, which implies a chosen lack of words.

### III

The exchange of bodies, not like exchanging prisoners, where all
are dressed in gray clothes, and their desire carries them across
the line to their lost country, not like that, an exchange of bod-
ies, a formal presentation of the lack of clothes, a formal pre-
sentation of skin, this hand rests above her head, clasping and
releasing what is invisible, the air, just like her clothes, left in
the hallway, left in a hurry, not wanting to be late for this formal
presentation of love, which has the ordered familiarity of hold,

then touch, then kiss, then touch lower, which has the formality of silence which implies a match, not like a small flame, but implies a match of silence, which is formal, like the exchange of letters, or of prisoners who long for their countries but cannot remember how to live there, once they cross the invisible line which divides the land, which feels like a wall one crosses over not knowing if there will be anyone there to meet, it has been years, dressed in old clothes, dressed in no clothes, not dressed, the hand resting on the white pillow, the hand touching the silent body, making a formal presentation of love, which implies a match, a lit cigarette, the time of gray light, which does not ease the formality of the presentation, which silence does not ease, which the hands do not ease, though they reach across white sheets, though one hand purified a needle once, lit a match once, wrote a letter once, more than once.

# Declaration of February

*The sun is heat to her now, and the sea, water.*
REBECCA HARDING DAVIS

I see what brings this on. Orion no longer threatens
to drop his three-starred dagger,
he's just some stars without configuration or danger,

and the green plants which once taught the daily lesson
of turning to the source of light now only demand
water and drop leaf after leaf, giving away their grace.

This is what happens when the veils of beauty
lift from love, and rapture lifts too, away from the heart,
leaving no love, no beauty, only revelation of the ordinary,

what is no longer needed. The sun recklessly enters all my
        windows
but it is the windows which speak of their own transparent design,
not the heat, not the light of a day.

Flowers are everywhere this winter, white daisies
spin out of remembered orbit, masculine iris arrowing
into a heart, Scottish daffodils once wild and abandoned

under my careless feet, and finally, the dark roses, which have
lived in the offices of my heart, and in the regained austerity
of my bedroom; they have no thorns and I let them die,

die some more, I do not let them go.
I see what brings this on, all the controlled flowering
in the mildest of winters, while the children fly by

on sleds down private hills, bring their exhaustion home,
divide me, join me, even they have faltered
during this winter discussion in my ordinary soul.

But they come upstairs, scissors
bright and bloodless, red paper, white arrows,
I love you and I like you, litany of childhood,

St. Valentine colliding with one birth, St. Valentine
of the broken, pierced clean through heart, celebrated
in red, who died like all saints, leaving nothing behind

but ritual. I will go near no ocean now, would not risk
such simple movement toward remembered joy, February
protects me with a winter sky, and the snow makes

the stars brighter, but less ordered. The days
and nights pass with little regard for safety,
and we are all separate starlight unable to diminish the dark.

# DIVORCE

*It takes long intimacy, long and familiar interliving,
    before one kind of creature can cause illness in
    another.*

    LEWIS THOMAS, *The Lives of a Cell*

When Bob called to read aloud to me that day in the office,
it felt just fine. I was busy being perfect in the old ways, shiny
armor, dull pain. I felt all right in my hard chair that protected
my back from the danger of too much gentleness. I think that
was the day we talked about the comfort of magazines, and
biographical notes in *Esquire*, that magazine for men and some
women. When he read to me about how unnecessary it was for
astronauts to be quarantined when they came home from the
moon I laughed, having always known intuitively that moon
germs would never cause my demise, so many other deaths read-
ily available. I kept smoking as he read, and when he got to the
line about "a long intimacy" I asked him to slow down, grabbed
my pencil, copied the sentence in fast hard letters. I remember
saying good-bye, picking up my children after work, fighting
with them in the grocery store about spending more quarters on
football helmet and chicken hatching machines, tucking them
in bed, and late that night throwing the quote into my notebook
labeled, "Poems by others, Quotations collected, Poems of mine
which other writers have worked on, Remember to Edit."

Now it feels like years later. I have trouble being perfect in public because my friends laugh so hard when I try. There has been so much correspondence, that graceful letter from Paulette, with a reminder to be proud, and my friend David telling me to remember that the first time I got on a bicycle it felt like the least natural thing to be doing with my sense of balance. I remember laughing in agreement, crying later. I did love my white bike so much, sold it to buy college books about geology and logic. Now I don't ride bikes with hand brakes, because when I was pregnant I came down a winding hill on a ten-speed bike, panicked, squeezed the brakes with my wet hands, and hurtled over the handlebars into a pond, landing between two swans who were stunned by my arrival.

I'd like to be proud of all the things I've resolved never to learn how to do, as if to prove that everything I know how to do is enough, and it's time to rest. I keep thinking of intimacy, and astronauts disappearing into the face of the moon. I was reminded by my friend Jim the other day that I thought I'd been divorced five years, but it had only been three. Then I was out buying my mother a valentine present, and I talked to the clerk about my son who was in fourth grade, and she said she'd assumed I was one of the college kids, out for a Saturday walk. So I came home and looked into the mirror for a while, remembering my mother's advice to start now with the face cream, before it's too late. I wanted to call out for blessings to descend into the hearts of all my friends. I wanted to drop to my knees and ask for something important for all of us who try to love carefully, who think too much, who try to stop our hands from breaking someone else's dreams, or from making shadows on someone else's face. There's that wild, holy feeling that comes over me; I never made it to my knees, but I thought about divorce, and intimacy, and illness, how it blossoms like splendid poisoned roses in all the story books. I wanted protection for everyone. I wanted all the astronauts to come home, leave the sky alone, to come out of quarantine and walk down ordinary roads, ridding themselves of weightlessness and the human desire to fly away from those we used to love.

# GRIEF

*Someone who is about to be left alone*
*Again, and can no longer stand it.*
              EDWARD HIRSCH, *Edward Hopper*
              *and the House by the Railroad (1925)*

This will have to stand for grief, this arrangement
outside my window, children playing that old statue game,
and the girl who's just no good at it.
When the leader yells "Freeze!" she's too liquid,
can't claim whatever shape she's hovering near.
I want to be that girl on the dark green lawn
who cannot hold her position. When you leave me
again my mouth will be open, screaming, my legs
running in your direction. And I don't even want
to stop you, only desire my composure shattered,
my body not held in check. I want to be calling
you back with all the codes broken, so you will
know the grief is alive and not considered.

# BELONGING TO GOD

Momentary exhilaration. You are fuller than your body can stretch, yet the skin holds. When my children belong to God I am caught by their easy giving over to ownership. My daughter calls from the bedroom that God has slipped his hand inside her red curtains, she tells me he's rearranged the dolls, the stuffed rabbit is mended, the ribbons have lost their knots, their tangled union. I'm in the kitchen and don't know what to do with the information. The knife doesn't slip. Dinner will be eaten on time, the time I say.

When my father talked of destiny I never thought of God, only of piano lessons arched over my life, umbrellas made of music, thought my fingers would always know the way to touch the white keys. I imagined baseball games I'd win alone, complacent champion, summer dust sifting into my tennis shoes, touching home. I thought of my brain cells multiplying in my skull, each new cell carrying truth, more lessons. I knew I needed all the facts there were to fulfill the luck of my own life.

My son called to me that God was inside his red fire engine. He wanted to show me. I did move as fast as I could, spilling like water through the kitchen door into a summer day, but God had left by the time I got there, my son smiled, told me I'd missed him by seconds.

Belonging to God took a lot of time when I was young. Praying right, the knot of fingers, hymns to be memorized, saying no to hot boy hands in backseats, trying to remember I belonged to God in those backseats took time.

Baptized at twelve, in white, the small of my back supported by a man's arm as he bent me backwards under water. It seemed like a sin to stand there in white, dripping on the carpet, it seemed like a sin not to feel I belonged to God when I went under the water like that, so many clothes on, my heart wide open and alert.

My daughter explained once, in the backseat of my car to her cousins, how to get God to come to you. "Two people sit very close, and they send their breaths into each other's mouths, back and forth, and their breaths get smaller and smaller and suddenly God is inside their mouths."

The music is strong today and everything seems sacred, the circles under my eyes, how green summer is, how rarely the sun shines these months, how rarely I go under water. Everything seems sacred, the hard music, my children belonging to God, how language tries to be correct, wants to be holy, fails, how music is the only thing I can stand under my skin, the only thing breaking into my heart, everything seems sacred, even not belonging to God feels sanctified.

# Folds of White Dress / Shaft of Light

*The Annunciation*
PETER PAUL RUBENS, 1577–1640


She had been reading, that much we know.
An empty vase beside her book, no one in this story
thought to bring her flowers.

The angel's cape is flame, his hair gold fire.
One more angel drops from heaven barefoot, the shoemakers sigh.
He is fine, and his gray wings match his outfit.
She is dressed for a dinner party and he flies through
the window, drops to his knee, beseeches her to accept
the offer. She listens but her hands are placed
on the canvas in shapes of rejection.

She would like to lift her eyes to the baby
angels floating near the ceiling.
She would like to catch the dove in her raised hand.
She may be glad the shaft of light turns her white dress
holy, she may not.

She worries: where can one place a beautiful man
angel at the dinner table, who can make small talk
with him, or offer polite inquiries about celestial weather?

She understands babies, even floating ones,
and she wants the dove to stay near her,
that much is clear, and it is also apparent
her blue cloak cannot protect her from god's
demand, or the strong hand reaching
toward her, about to make her famous
and pregnant.

# BE GOOD

*It is not hard for one to do a bit of good. What is*
*hard is to do good all one's life and never do*
*anything bad.*

MAO TSE-TUNG

Today I heard a story about a priest,
and watched my children be good for hours,
and I was good too, and felt goodness
taking its usual toll, felt the old ambivilance
slide under my skin.

Today I heard a story about a priest,
a good priest who went when called,
to old parishoners, to crazy bishops,
with no care he kept going, always pulled
from bed or prayer, coming and going too many times
a day, for goodness, and he gave that goodness away
until his good heart broke open and he died, good and young.

Today I felt like being bad for many weeks,
wanted my children to watch me, these children,
destined to be good, wanted to sweep that goodness
out of them, feeling the old tracks they're on are
too set, too shiny for them to ever step off.

Today I thought of childhood girlfriends, Lori, Kathy, Kristine,
all of us brought up on *Little Women*, how all of us would,
after the Beatles records were put away at night,
talk about goodness, and sometimes beauty and goodness,
and which we would choose if we could only have one.

Be good, I say to my children every day, never telling
them to be beautiful, though they are both.
Be good, I say to myself, good like a priest,
be good in huge swirls of time, year after year
of sweeping, spinning canvases of goodness, yes,
be good today because badness has such energy
it can drive the goodness from your soul
and leave you bad, even if you've practiced
goodness, and have been walking down the road
to grace all your life.

# GOOD DREAMS OR MILK

*Still impossible to kiss the child,*
*and not see the child explode.*
                    CHARLES BAXTER, *Cantata At Midnight*


private retreats and public disorders
are in full view now; after a long season
without new life babies ride inside friends
or burn whole into lives, altering paths we'd been lingering on.

there are mouths to feed. my children's faces
are private candles i sometimes worship at, the touch of
their skin, the implicit blessing that comes when children
are desired, and children are being born again, while the world
lurches in a fouled orbit, tampering with private pledges
made in the night by new lovers, and with lullabies being sung
all over town:
                pony boy, pony boy, won't you be my pony boy?
                and:
                sweet and low, sweet and low, winds of western seas.
the hush hush words about mockingbirds,
rings without stain,
soft words before sleep,
the comfort of new skin and old songs.

such privacy by gold light cannot outshine the polished guns,
the accomplished liars, the diplomats flaming at the last gates
in every city, easter won't stay, palm fronds fade
and children's new clothes are put away with trembling hands
by lovers who bend to kiss the faces of children,
or to hear the daughter's voice: oh, i've needed you so much
today, weary, as if laying claim to some sin.

and the big world's chapter and verse drone on,
and children are flying apart
and hands cannot reach
fast enough to stop their small, quiet disintegration.

we are here again, we say to each other,
while the children tangle in sheets,
call out for good dreams or milk,
and we pull the blankets up, hungry for them
to wake up alive.

# What He Liked
# He Had a Lot Of

*For Dick Francis*

Ushered into the backyard, you see one thousand
peonies, one thousand for sure, at least, only pink,
and she raises her hand in an arc, and her arm bends
like the stem of a peony under the weight of bloom,
she says: what he liked he had a lot of.
Though he died many years ago, no other flowers
have been added to this hidden English garden.
It's too many to praise, too many to ignore.

She takes you inside and you don't say a word:
every space on every wall holds a painting
of a sailing ship, or, many sailing ships,
or ships in harbor, or a ship at sunset.
"Oh, look," you say, "here's a ship up on shore."
Painted men are repairing it, high noon and glossy.

She takes you out through the backyard,
the interview complete, lets you out the gate,
her eyes ride your sloping shoulders down
the old street.

So many blossoms, so many sailing ships;
the world feels cramped and unsteady.
You walk quickly, claustrophobic, your stomach
at sea without you, the peony in your lapel
full-blown and gaudy, a tiny clown's wig
riding on your breast, you, the one who's
never liked more than one of anything.

# THE TREES

*For Pat and Tim*

(When the little girl was asked, "And what do you like best
about the State Fair?" she said, "The trees.")

Winners in beauty, in talent, in patient congeniality.
The trees stay up, the trees change colors, the trees grow
and make rings to wear for birthdays.
This tree bears fruit, this tree breaks the heart, this tree
opens all eyes to possibilities.
This tree won the amateur talent contest
      singing *Flow Gently Sweet Afton*.
This tree won for beauty, the judges rooted to their chairs,
a unanimous ballot.
This tree was a friend, turned his back on jealousy,
      gave shade in the heat wave.
The trees at the fair avoid games of chance and never travel.
The trees at the fair are quiet, the horses and lop-eared rabbits
watch them from the open air barns; they can never meet.
The trees at the fair have green hearts, open hands, they wait
and watch, they own nothing, they are not prideful, they make no
false moves, they bend away from neon, they do not know how
to love themselves, they love the girl who loves the trees.

# The Amateur

*Whenever a celebrated murder occurred Bolden*
*was there at the scene drawing amateur maps.*
*There were his dreams of his children dying.*
*There were his dreams of his children dying.*
*There were his dreams of his children dying.*
MICHAEL ONDAATJE,
*Coming Through Slaughter*

In seventh grade geography we colored maps.
The continent of Africa was assigned when I
was in my red period. Each exotic country
challenged my crayons, my sense of harmony.
Cardinal red, plum, violet for the African
flowers on my mother's window ledge, wine,
the dark continent blossomed under my
steady left hand. Never before have so
many stars risen at the top of my work.
A true amateur, I colored for love.

An amateur parent at twenty-one, I was in
my blue period, to match my son's eyes and
the heaviness in my heart. His infant kabuki
hands defined the air, my dreams grew unsteady
as he grew more beautiful. I charted elaborate
plans for my life without him, while he dreamt

145

of clowns coming through the window to scratch
his eyes, and so we painted clowns, coloring
in details of anonymous faces, red stars on
flat white cheeks, blue triangles over empty
eyes. He slept easier then, while I dreamt
of masked men pushing him through the bedroom
window after disconnecting the stereo, severing
the telephone cord.

When my daughter in her dark beauty arrived
I longed for hours of dream-filled sleep,
but she upset the mapping out I did for her
future with illness, her unsteady breathing
became the rhythm of my nights, for a year
all nights were broken, and she and I did
the rocking chair dance and far away in Africa
civil wars changed the names of half the countries
I had colored, believing they would never be altered.

It doesn't matter how many scientists explore
the country of sleep. It doesn't matter that
police draw white chalk lines around bodies
violently dispatched to eternity. Nothing
defines absence, there are no colors to choose
from when drawing in the shapes of missing
children, and when they slip away as you hold them,
or disappear under car wheels, or swim too far
in your dreams of water there are no rescues
plotted, the god of dreams is malevolent,
a professional, and you have done it all
for love, the competition is fixed, and the dream
of death is the first blossom after a child
blooms under your skin.

# Admission

*For Stephen*

## I

Nothing prepared me for the surprise
of longing for you. Just fly east, I thought,
to the breaking edge of America, find some sun,
and the old comfort of silence and the empty bed.
Fly east, not so far as China, just far enough away
from acknowledged love,
the fierce uncertainties.

## II

Sometimes I think I'm a hard person,
harsh in spirit and language,
always breaking fast for the Atlantic
where nothing matters except sand,
where nothing matters but the search
for white stones, and the children

who skim past in waves: my only work
to catch them from the white foam before the tide
forces them to face the ocean, not the dunes.

## III

I can hold children in my hands,
I can slip white stones into pockets,
I can walk the bay side, quiet life in tide pools,
I can walk the ocean side, shuddering with solitude,
its dark complications.
I can do all this, and sleep alone, my body in fever
from too much sun, my eyes sorry to give up the light,
the half-read book.
I know all these things, the accomplishments
of a private life, yet the discovery
that you had come east with me
caught me up short, left me without breath.

Sometimes I think I know everything I want.
This time I was wrong, and admit without complacency
that the memory of your mouth turned my heart
like a red shell cast up
by the one wave I could not resist swimming in.

# Greenland Mummy

The best preserved of all the Greenland mummies is the baby boy
mummy. He died quickly at six months of age, the snow his
bed, his blanket, his death. So intact, he takes the breath of the
archeologists: two white shells — lower teeth, cornsilk for hair,
his tiny gloves, little blue starfish in the snow.

I make so much up. Haven't the time to study properly. I
read two pages, pronounce a novelist "psychotic." I read one
paragraph and know more than I ever wanted to know about
the Greenland mummies.

The baby mummy wasn't wearing gloves; no shells, no corn-
silk, a baby, not a doll. He was given to the snow after his mother
died, so he couldn't wear gloves or the beautiful red over-alls or
the soft deerskin cap with ear flaps, I made all that up when I was
painting the baby mummy, I made it up so he would be warm.

Given to the snow because his mother died. The old rules
hurt, not that the new rules are ideal. When the mother died
in Greenland so many hundreds of years ago then her baby was
put outside to die. And he became the best mummy, the one
the scientists loved the best, because his little body froze so
quickly, more quickly than the grown-up mummies and teen-age
mummies who died with their clothes on. It is good he froze so
quickly because the scientists are able to learn more from his
tiny body. It is good to freeze quickly when your mother dies.

It is good the rule was so clear: no aunts, no best friends of the mother may take the child; it is good to sleep in the snow when your mother dies. Maybe your aunt wouldn't love you enough, maybe your mother's best friend would love her own baby more. Who thought of such a dramatic rule in a country named Greenland? Who thought of Greenland anyway, that name of life, that huge island, and who thought of digging for mummies in the first place?

I don't know these answers. I don't read much lately, except what's assigned or what I struggle to see beyond the veil of tiredness. The baby wakes at night and I can't get back to sleep. I am sitting outside his door, my back straight against the doorframe. I am listening to each ragged breath he takes this month. I don't read much because of the baby. The baby is why I make things up. I love being up in the middle of the night with him; we watch the news, or old David Niven movies. We watched *Hawaii*, saw the circle of white, the halo/aura around Julie Andrews' head after she screamed and pulled on the tied-in-knots bedsheet and had her first baby. That is the first scene I ever remember seeing of childbirth. Later, a baby is put in the beautiful ocean to drown. I turned the TV off then because Joey was falling asleep. I wouldn't have let him watch that scene anyway.

The snow is almost gone from our backyard. My daughter made a mermaid without a face, with purple yarn hair; only the hair and the last part of the flipping tail remain. My daughter wants to be a mermaid when she grows up. Our baby will never sleep in the snow. I won't even let him go winter camping, even if it's the only way he can win merit badges in Boy Scouts. The baby will keep his snuggie on, and his blue mittens from Aunt Peggy, and his dark blue snowsuit from Jean, and his Harlequin socks from Pat and Tim, and the baby will sleep indoors always unless we move to the tropics.

The Greenland baby mummy has a beautiful and haunting face. I keep thinking of him, his small face, how he would fit in the hands and arms and heart of his mother who died.

I have been in mourning for children all over the world since our baby was born six months ago. The news from China, Africa, Lebanon; you can't send money fast enough, you can't melt the snow fast enough, or turn down the sun, or grow the crops or stop the bombs fast enough. Our new baby has done his job well, the job all babies are assigned: he has broken open my heart for the third time in my life, he has made me think of all these babies, alive, dead and dying. This is the work of babies; that is why there's no time to read, why I make everything up as I go along.

They are searching for more Greenland mummies. The group graves are confusing to the archeologists, so they hope to find more single graves. If they're lucky, they will stumble across another Greenland mummy baby. They hope the next one they find will have died even faster than the first. They long for what the snow does to babies.

That part may be wrong. They may have left Greenland by now. I will not be going to Greenland this year. I carry the picture of the baby mummy deep in me, like something I swallowed that has nothing to do with food. One paragraph, one picture is enough. Our baby is sleeping right now. He is warm, getting over his ailments of the last month. He is the light in our house. Someday I will tell him all these stories, the sad ones, the famines, the girl children left out to die, and the happy ones, the mermaid in the backyard, the women who love him, the gifts they've given. I am glad winter is ending and that the snow is almost gone.

# HAPPINESS

# Small History

*She said it, she said,*
*"If I can't say something truthful*
*then I'm not going to talk."*

PATRICIA WEAVER FRANCISCO

I am going to make myself a small history. I am going to tell
and not show, show and not tell.

The smallness will be its beauty. There's a girl whose oldest
brother's dogs always died violently. Can you see her brother

walking up the dead-end street, another golden dog dead in his
arms, and the mother says, "He must have gotten into the

neighbor's poison." The boy is crying hard. He probably should
cry this hard every couple of months but the girl doesn't think

he's cried in years. The girl thinks the neighbors keep poison
and she still thinks that. This is history.

This small girl never had a dog that was her dog until it was
almost too late to love dogs the way her brother did.

When she finally got a dog she had to leave town, she flew all
the way to Athens, then in the middle of the night she got on

the smallest plane in the sky and went to an island to live.
She was sixteen and her dog was back home. She didn't think

about the dog at all, but in an old letter her mother saved
she sees her erratic teenage handwriting—"Give Garf a pat

for me." Named for Garfunkel. Now that dog is dead, but she
gave him away long before to a man whose job it was to

walk all the parks and protected forests in her hometown.
He was just supposed to walk and notice things. Her dog was

happy. On this island so many years ago a man told her she was
beautiful. Another man held her hand every night at the outdoor

movie theater where she watched *Suddenly Last Summer* dubbed
in Greek, and crazy Italian movies dubbed in Greek,

and really, she saw the worst movies she'd ever seen that
summer, under stars that were huge and fell constantly.

On the island so many years ago one man gave her a necklace
with a silver madonna swinging from the chain, and another

man gave her flowers every day at the same cafe where she sat
writing letters home, reading, while everyone else slept

the hot afternoons away. She calls this her summer of men.
How strange they were to love her, adore her, make up pet

names for her. To her mother, as a baby she'd been an object
of beauty, the desired girl, she has always understood that.

On the island, to be purely an object of desire in a summer
of ecstatic heat and sunlight—she felt holy and carnal.

She has saved her paintings from that time, timid brushstrokes,
the perfect reflection of her fear and desire waking at once.

The father of the family who petted her in her sleep, and when
she woke to his strokes he said, "Shshshshshsh."

The young revolutionaries who told her to swim far out into the
Aegean so they could tell her in broken English about the junta,

the older brother imprisoned, the cousin disappeared, would she
carry the word back home to her America?

"Yes," she said, but no one cared too much when she did, such a
small disturbance on the planet, and Vietnam claimed the light

when she got off the airplane and was American again. She has
this picture in her mind of her middle brother telling her to

read *The Stranger*. She is twelve and she reads all night. The
kind of heat in that book is what she finds when she arrives

in Corfu four years later. She did not believe in that kind of
heat until she felt it on her skin. Did she think Camus was

a liar? No, she had only thought the word "fiction." She is
desperately attracted to that kind of heat. Later, when she

spends a year living in Scotland, she cannot believe it never
gets warm. Somewhere she'd decided that crossing an ocean

meant access to heat. In the middle of the most beautiful
country she is inconsolable; there is nothing warm in Scotland

except her home. She shakes with the cold in other people's
houses. She weeps when she goes out walking, the fog and mist

are furry, she feels pressed with all this moisture, her body
fat with cold and damp. After she read Camus all those years

ago she knew she would never kill anyone. But in Scotland,
after she gives birth to her first son, she admits she will

kill anyone who tries to harm this new child. She accepts
this as a reasonable change of heart. In Corfu, all the heat

got tangled up with all the desire and all the beauty, and
because she was called beautiful she decided the heat made her

that way. In Scotland, she wears the same dress for months.
It is a pale, apple-green color. She has wanted to describe

this dress, its true color, for half her life now. It is not
enough to say "apple-green." It is not enough to add the word

pale. Now she spends time trying to paint the color of this
corduroy dress. She searches art stores for the right colored

pencil, the right tube of paint. She cannot believe she will
have to work to make a color she remembers so clearly. When

she was pregnant she could not eat. Finally, all she could
eat were Granny Smith apples; she was so grateful to be able

to eat those green apples and not throw up. She keeps bowls
of them in her home. They become holy objects, she believes

the baby did not die inside her because she could finally
eat something and it stayed eaten. These apples are not

quite the color green she is searching for. It seems to her
that farmers keep changing the color of Granny Smith apples.

She thinks they are using new chemicals and that the color
and taste are being altered. She does not know where the

beautiful, incredibly soft pale apple-green corduroy dress
is any more. She thinks for a moment she would get pregnant

again if only she could wear that dress again for nine months.
She writes some lines of dialogue for her new novel. The

woman says, "That's the whole point. I hate this cat, but the
cat will die and I'll have to cry and I'll have to bury it

and I won't even have liked the cat and I'll have this whole
set of feelings anyway and that's what I hate." And the man

says, "I don't get it." I never meant to write in the third
person. I woke up one morning and I wanted to start telling

the truth about parts of my life that I never talk about. I
barely believe my life was ever like any of this. It's

unbearably cold today, and yesterday, and the day before
yesterday. My husband's car kind of blew up last Saturday

and I could only laugh. And I read Joyce Johnson's book,
*Minor Characters*, and got so mad all over again about women

in this culture, women without names, without acknowledgment.
This morning I am thinking about telling the truth and I am

a little cold. There is this path we all think about walking
down toward our future, this path we already walked on. That's

all I can think about, this path, this road that is one perfect
straight line even if it goes around the world through heat

and fog and rain and snow and it's my life I keep thinking.

It's my life.

# ALONE

Not so bleak today.
She's alone but
not alone.
There are children.
In their early perfection
she sought her image.
Mistakes were made;
she punished herself
over and over again.

The therapist asked her
daughter: Is your mother
needy?

"No."

That was the point.
Be useful or die.

Did her own mother need her?
Yes, but she has a life,
still. Still, the need
holds her in place.

The children are themselves.
Wasn't this the only purpose?
She said, "I don't worry about you,"
to the oldest son, who said,
"I worry about you."

The oldest daughter said:
"She just doesn't get it.
I don't worry. Worry's stupid."
It all feels pretty stupid lately.
Mortal, yes, she's mortal every day
now, staring in her face in the real
mirror.

Her body's alive. She can feel the motor
running down. She doesn't want
to abandon anyone too early, but she might.
Sometimes walking up the stairs she thinks—
now. She doesn't want
to die in any way she can imagine.
She has a large imagination but it's no longer
a comfort to her.

# ARCHITECTURE

My father's calling from the bottom of the stairs,
the angry god I've enraged by not picking up
the dish towel fast enough.
Looking down at his face I think I see his vocal cords
drumming inside his throat. Is that my name he's saying?

Looking down he's all face, the roaring mouth,
not god, never god, not king of the garden,
never king of my heart.

In those small moments in his life when sanctimony replaces
vodka, the children are laid on altars, but the prayers
can't go high enough. Then he's despairing, disconnected,
destroyed. There's no vertical energy to his longing.

Up and down the stairs, positions of poverty and power.
I was upstairs, waiting to be summoned, no way out
except down and through what I'd climbed to avoid.

When my brother brought the bottle down on my father's head
and the hallway was bright with glass and blood
I never imagined a straight path through, couldn't see
how to step over his forlorn and broken spirit.

His brilliance never made any light, and oh, the burden
children feel to make light. "I'll be a sunbeam for Jesus,"
and "You are my sunshine, my only sunshine." Do I sing
those songs to my children? Songs full of personal poison,
and these innocent songwriters are clueless as they're inventing,
and these parents, innocent, too,
keep making these neutral and beautiful babies,
and then they keep them.

# THE FATHERS WALKING
# AWAY FROM HOUSES

*For JoAnn Verburg*

The fathers walk away from the houses.
We're just girls so maybe we don't see at first
how their shoulders lift, burdens slipping into green
grass, or maybe we notice they walk more smoothly.
The fathers go out side doors or back doors;
they have work to do in the green backyards.

They pick up rakes or trowels; one father
carries new bedding plants meant for shade.
Now he is planting impatiens, now he says,
"Don't be this flower. Don't be impatiens."

Our fathers walk away, and we're girls so maybe
it seems as if they are moving through
a leafy green tunnel, and we already know
they will return to the houses lighter, more lift
in their legs, backs calm and straight.

The fathers walk away from the houses.
The voices of the women and girls don't carry down
the green lawns, and the birds at the crowns
of trees don't speak in feminine song.

We're just girls, and we want our fathers
to be happy. We help them down the steps,
out the door, we tell them, "Walk away
from the house." The fathers carry tools and flowers,
carry green snake hoses and silver buckets.
The fathers do their silent work in the darkening green,
and we tell them, "Come home before night."

# WHEN THE DEAD COME
# TO VISIT IN DREAMS

They have questions about placement.
"Where have you assigned me? How many memories are left?"
My father asks if I remember his early beauty.
He asks, "Are you happy?" but is gone before I can think
of the answer he wants, the answer I have.

In the first dream he sleeps in his bed.
My mother sends me in to wake him, I cup my small hand
around the curve of his shoulder, I touch his breathing
waist, I call, "Dad, Dad, it's time to wake up,"
but he sleeps on. I put my mouth to his dreaming ear
and say good-bye.

My mother, standing in the doorframe of the same dream
tells me to take his car and leave. Driving away
in my father's white Studebaker I am so happy. I call
back over my shoulder to say, "Yes, I'm happy,"
then remember the question comes from another dream.

My friend asks if I'm famous, if I've had more children.
When I tell her—another son—she says in her dream voice,
"I hope the new one is quiet. You need some quiet."

When the dead come to visit in dreams they are deeply curious
but disinterested in some holy, unexpected ways.
Most times it doesn't matter what I answer. I can say,
"You're an angel in my sky." I can say, "Dad, I miss you."

I can tell them all this while I'm dreaming, or
on the freeway the next morning, frost past the danger point,
the road a collective illusion. I tell them
I love them. I tell them anything I want.

When the dead come to visit me at night they take some part
of my heart away, as if it's part of some celestial puzzle
they are working on, but they always
bring my heart back to me, and I wake up
lonely, and relieved by their absence.

# Fox

I saw a fox, red as a small sunset on cloudless horizon.
Red as flame is supposed to be. It's my childhood

dream: I thought fox traveling fast, fox roaming past
me, intent on his life, thought smaller nose, rounder face,
I thought no teeth, no curled back lip.

When I was small, animals stayed smaller than me. Books
I lived in controlled the dream sizes.

I didn't want to write about the fox dragging the small
rabbit across the road, rabbit dying not dead. It doesn't
matter, one less rabbit. Just another golden book

for the children of foxes. The line of blood was never
in my dream, not that red, not that path.

A friend called to me, said the lop-eared rabbit
in the cage looked like my oldest daughter. "Don't you think
this beautiful rabbit looks like Molly?"

Maybe the eyes, I might have said, the eyes, yes, green
as the weakening forest, no, in the dream it was green
as the wakening forest.

When I was a child no one was telling the story
I ended up living. I was in the forest once. It is so hard
to send my daughters in.

# LIVING

I am living the life of the body one last time with the new
baby. I watch CNN all day and night. When she was brand
new, I watched the beginning of the slaughter in Liberia.
The reporter said, "The victims are mostly women, their heads
taken off, their babies still strapped to their backs.
Dead babies hung from the backs of the dead women.
Many women were murdered in the window frames as they tried
to escape from the church they'd gone to for sanctuary."

Today my safe white body smelled of milk and pizza. My oldest
son wept in my arms; he'd just come off a twelve hour shift
driving the pizza truck. If a friend calls, I ask what day
it is. My oldest son says, "They'll never catch me, mom. And
they say you can come home after seven years." I think of
Tranströmer, the grass whispering amnesty, how many years I've
carried the poem in my heart. My heart pounds and wakes the
baby.

Liberia was created by Africans who so despised their lives of
slavery in America they returned across the ocean to be free.
It is months later now; today's weather report says heavy fog
in St. Paul, heavy fog in Baghdad. Regular human beings are
praying and singing, regular human beings have been carrying
candles and praying for peace.

My little son has learned to move through the neighborhood
without me. He has crossed his first streets, his first alleys
without me. When we brought the baby home Joey looked huge,
I sat and tried to remember the size of his skull when he
was born, but now his head looked enormous, almost mutant.
His perfect eyes seemed too large. His beautiful arms and legs
giant appendages, inappropriate and looming next to Cordelia's
immense smallness. My mother says, "Don't you just love a
baby's hands?" Yes, I do.

Here in the world I feel crazy possessing a regular life. My
oldest son says, "Who are the four people who will write my
letters, saying my way has always been the way of peace?" A
year ago I let my cynical nature slip, wept as the wall went
down. Now the new baby is a few months old. My four children
came from my body loving peace, but I cannot protect them
with the war stories that invade my poems.

# BURNING

*"Control nature," my father said.*
*Or: "We must get this yard under control."*
*I think that's right.*


I thought of myself as doing the best I could.
Filling buckets, carrying them, aching fingers
coiled around metal, down the slope,
one bucket for each new tomato plant.
I first made a moat for each green life.
I tilted the lip of the bucket
and the moats filled. I watched the stalks lift,
the green veins fill.

Now there's other conversation.
My son says, "Could you do that in the olden days?"
And I say, "Yes, we could burn and burn and no one cared."
What city friends never understand—not just the leaves
of autumn burned, but in March and April we burned
a line across the back acres, getting rid
of last year's stubble, burning the volunteers
my father hadn't planted himself.

Now I know I was too young to be left
in charge of a line of fire. Where did he go
that spring day, leaving me with a rake,
a hose that didn't stretch far enough?

I think he went for a drink, a bottle hidden
in the rose bushes, or maybe for another nap of oblivion;
then I only felt he'd given me a precious job.
I don't remember feeling small until the fire jumped
in the wind, and my rake, my anxious movements couldn't hold
the heat in place.

It doesn't matter. The yard survived, though fire took
the raspberry patch, three pines, the best oak for climbing.

I see my son and daughter think I'm old, a pioneer
who believed in burning for free, a sky that could abide
smoke and forever be clean.

The yard's rearranged now. One tornado, two straight line
wind storms, two brothers, one girl, handy neighbors
carrying spring promises. The willows my father planted
still grow in the next yard, land sold off
when his job was taken from him.
He controlled nothing, finally, but the patient
and decisive movement of his body into the path
of a train.

What jobs are right for children?
I give my daughter no line of fire
to guard. I ask too little, I think,
and worry they will never be serious enough
for the world.

I stand now under the willows, knowing they root faster,
grow farther, lift higher than any other tree I might choose
for my plot of city land. My father said,

"You plant a willow, and you'll still be around
to see it tower over you."

# LOVING MOTELS

Feels American.
Shameless, somehow.
People I don't know
love motels. People
I don't know love chlorine;
hundreds and thousands of people
I know and don't know
love motel pools, whirlpools,
hot tubs, saunas.
People I love, people who love
me, those people love room service.
The sheer
intellectual weight: the idea of a phone,
wires, another phone, then food arriving.
Preposterous and sexual.
Sexy, like those bathing suits
you only wear in pools
in motels in Montreal, or
pools in Shawnee Mission, any pool
where no one you know will walk by
and know you.
Loving motels means loving
what has not rooted in your spirit.

Loving motels is loving
your very own ice bucket,
and the special shapes the ice takes,
is loving the shining cans of pop
sinking through the melting ice,
the sound aluminum makes
while you pretend to sleep,
is loving the hidden air conditioners
and the cable TV shows, and is
letting no one else, not even someone
you love, use your own wrapped
bar of soap, or your own little pack
of ten-month-old Sanka
or the sweet little hot plate
that just fits the baby coffee pot.
People like me and including me
love motels for the white towels
which remind us of something large
we have lost somewhere. We love
the deep shag carpet we would hate
at home. We love the key,
the number, the simple locks,
not like home where locks are hard,
needing a hip thrown against
the door, the dead bolt really dead,
we love the simple key with the simple
plastic shape: sometimes a fish,
sometimes a smooth, beige oval,
sometimes, if we're lucky,
a shamrock, a clover, a doll or dog.
We love motels for letting us
drive up, we get our own parking place

automatically, then we get love-
making that is not connected
to our own bed's history,
and besides the white towels
we get white sheets
which we all love and never buy.
We get left alone,
we get the feeling of being alone,
and we need America to leave us
alone in the motels.

# ROGUE WAVE

In Miami, that exotic
land, the Rogue Wave
came from nowhere
the meteorologists
swear, nowhere,
traveled seventy-five
feet without effort
crossing the boundary
of beach, of good taste,
of rules the tourists
thought they were living
by. That wave came
at night, wise wave
full of water smarts
and didn't carry away
any moon bathers, just
swept a three-year-old's
hand from her mother's
while they were
standing outside
a convenience store
at 11:30 at night,
and the mother said

something like, I just
planted my feet and
opened my arms as wide
as I could and prayed
the wave was on a straight
path and would bring
my child back to me.
And the wave in its
kindness did return
the child alive,
brought the child
with force and precision
into the open body
of the mother.
The Rogue Wave took
several kiosks out
to sea, and many
racks of T-shirts,
and hundreds of pairs
of plastic thongs
which later sharks
with bad eyesight
thought were small
neon-colored carp.
The Rogue Wave
complicated so
few lives that
it has been forgotten
except by
the mother, who swims
now each day, who
never liked the water

before it gave
back her daughter,
except by
the daughter, who churns
in her blankets each night,
swept away, over
and over again,
panicked and lost,
free, then held
by human arms.

# Why They Belong Together

In this cemetery coyotes and jackals mate. Their babies glisten
in full summer sun. I am not afraid of these helpless babies,
only their parents, teeth full of moonlight.

Buddha, so huge in your peacefulness. I could not pray
to anyone so untormented. Your dreams are simple; you do not
even fall asleep to have them.

I believe in justice, struggle to commit more than good manners
and my children's upbringing to that slippery word.

The Buddha doesn't care, but he's clear about that. I would fly
past him in a helicopter. I would touch his golden face with
my human hand. I would give him anything.

In the graveyard I cannot find the few stones I am searching for.
When my mother dies, I am to move my father's ashes to her grave
in Salt Lake City. The lawyer said, "Plan ahead. You need three
separate permits to move him." I told him my father has always
been lots of work, but I've had years of rest. The only real
question is: will either of them know if I don't do my job?

My baby's arms are outstretched with passion toward the dog
coming down the street toward us. Clearly he could take her face
off before I could stop him, but she offers herself up, her face
a pond for every dog she embraces.

Right now, the idea of sunlight seems foreign, as if the sun
never sent me into rapture.

Buddha, my hand touches your left eye, and there is still room
for many other hands before we could block your sight, halfway.
But I am by myself, in natural light, and I suddenly do not want
to touch you at all.

# COMFORT

*"We have everything we need to believe*
*right here in front of us."*
DABNEY STUART

I put my mouth on the wound of the tree.
I breathed, a child in my father's yard.
My breath was a Valentine, came from my red heart.

The tree lived long past the time of its wound.
My father went to his grave, and I believed in his death.
In the yard I would do his work, taught my children his name.

My mother inside the window watched us
and we turned to wave, her love for us involuntary,
streaming through the glass; she held her position.

My oldest son said, high in the branches of the tree,
"Here are his arms, I am swinging from his arms."
The tree turned to me, promised to live until I could do

without him.

# What It Was Like Today

I was studying at the dining room table and looked out the front
window. Saw my car parked on the street, metal proof I was
home. Reading Audre Lorde, reading Frank O'Hara, taking too
many notes.

The other night my oldest son was awake half the night
though I did not know it until morning. He'd been afraid to
call out to us for fear of waking his baby brother, and afraid to
leave his room because in his dream the werewolves were at his
door, and he had seen another one perched on his window sill.
He had a long night, though I heard him laughing about it with
a friend soon enough. This morning, driving him to school, he
said, "white people" with such disgust I burst out laughing. We
had been talking about Martin Luther King, about how much
history I'd lived through.

Today, when I saw my car on the street I admitted I was
part of history, that I was positioned, that my heart was home,
that my children's hearts were at that very moment beating
in three different places, white children, and I thought of my
daughter making a Martin Luther King board game for an
assignment. Playing the game with her stepdad one night I
heard him laugh because he got ten points for knowing the

first name of King's first child, but only four points for knowing where King delivered his "I Have A Dream" speech. I listened to him try to explain that it was what King did that mattered more than the name of his child, so he thought her point system was flawed.

Last night all my children died in a specific way in my dream. Around four AM the war I keep waiting for finally arrived and I was sitting on our old couch which my son insults each day, the dreadful brocade pattern, the hideous green and turquoise colors, and somehow I was holding all three of them in my arms, watching TV in some dreadful parody of the ways we watch TV, listening to the announcement that the bombs were flying, were falling, and as I sat there each child turned to vapor, turned to dust and ash in my arms, and I remember thinking in my dream that it was terrible to be holding some thing substantial, like flesh, like the silken feel of children's skin, or the feel of the baby's corduroy overalls against my wrist, and then to feel my children as dust, utterly dry, the beautiful blood absent, the liquid eyes dust, their three differently shaped mouths dust, their Dr. Who T-shirts dust, I remember thinking: where are they? and in the dream I wept to be left alive, sitting on the damn couch trying to get their dust off my hands, the texture was like cleaning the vacuum cleaner, dirty and absolutely dry, and then I woke and thought of snow never falling, rain never falling, tears never falling, thought of each child having one bath a day, needing all that water, thought of water fountains in three schools, thought of them.

I was grateful to wake from my dream, but today I am sick of myself in some special way, ashamed that I let my children go to their schools, that I did not answer the power of the dream by keeping their warm flesh and blood around me today, but I didn't keep them home, and I will not sit on the couch with all three of them again for a long, long time, the long long time I want to be their lives, not all four of us on the couch, not for a long and dreamless time.

# LILACS AND HAIL

*For Cheryl Miller and Will Powers*

The air's midwestern. There's this one perfect
month. First forsythia breaks open along the bark,
yellow petals shaped like small mussel shells, and
then the lilacs begin, first the ordinary lavender,
drenching the air with sweetness, then two days later
the white lilacs that brides and children sleep with.

A pause, and then the French lilac opens, and then
it just stays. That's what we meant to write you.
We tore armfuls from the tree, and it never showed,
and the scent was lyric, from the middle of the country.

Before the bridal's wreath in its curves, before the
sand cherry tree with its starlight blossoms, during
the wild flowering of the crabapple trees, that's when
the hail fell from the sky, and our street was a steel
drum band, each car hood a different pitch depending
on the quality of the tin, or the quality of the hail.

We came out of our houses. The earth is so dry here, and
the hail stones melted into the green lawns so quickly,
like a hard worker racing through dinner, like the grass
needed the hail to hold onto its green, so the hail came

like music and everyone was laughing. Then the sky
cleared, two rainbows jazzed up the sky, people got shier
and left their front porches.

The air's so sweet. There's one month when the possibility
of paradise seems to live in every alley, and the Hmong kids
and the black kids and the white kids are playing
basketball, and their spring jackets decorate
the lilac trees, and we fall asleep to the sound of the
basketballs bouncing in the alley, to the sound of the hoop
letting the ball fall in the scent of the night.

# Night Walk

The last lover you had before your first marriage
called a few weeks ago.
You felt the heat.
When he asked about old friends you'd known
in common you said, "Being with you, all I remember
is a dark circle; we didn't even have each other
in common."

That interested him, neither of you moonlight
for the other; you could read his swift intake of breath
over the wires.

He said, "I think we must live near each other. The phone
caught so quickly, the ring, I mean."

You thought of voodoo, his pale blue eyes,
sixteen years of silence.

And then you started running, not walking,
and a girl stood on the hood of her car at Hamline and Summit
screaming, "Don't hurt my car, you assholes."
Holding a ray-gun, a pitchfork in her hand.

You started running because people are frightening,
except for kind lovers, or your husband, "the kindest man
who ever loved you."

Your old lover lives close by, you'd assumed him dead
in Central America, underground in D.C., but you have
walked past his house for two years now without knowing.

Now you avoid his street, the simple code of his address.
Who can you live with in a circle of light?

A car goes by and you believe the silver bike
tied to the top is a Christmas tree.
You haven't even noticed the moon,
though it hangs, a perfect circle in the sky.

You see two lovers embracing near the stand of crabapple trees.
You feel huge as you run past them, bodiless and gigantic
with your double shadow.

You're close to home now; the moon becomes real.
Your lover said, "I guess we'll see each other
when we're supposed to."

The phone is light in your hands,
nothing is casual enough.

This lover was disembodied for so long,
the myth you never put down,
how he died in Nicaragua,
how the ashes blew your way,
and you caught his hand, his heart.

You told your friend this week,
"Let the young man go who killed himself.
You slow him down by thinking his light
is still around. You slow down his journey
with your anger. Let him go to heaven
with the gunshot in his temple, the third eye,
the last circle."

You are running down Summit Avenue in the dark:
harmony and the moon and the screaming girl.

The woman in your dream says,
"It was an accident in my life.
Give me a candy bar.
Give me your baby for my loving toy.
Honey, give me that baby and let's see
the Christmas tree now. I like the light
on the silver threads."

I can live with the kindest man who ever loved me.
I can run the streets of my city in the perfect air
that surrounds my life.
Trains still frighten me, and the dark circle we lived in,
that too, and I can speak with this voice as I run,
but I hear the young woman speaking from the single bed,
from the small room she almost got lost in
so many years ago, she says,

"You break my heart
in the moonlight.
You fill me with such desire.
I am afraid of you. Hold me."

# Amnesia Plague

You thought it was only you. You couldn't remember the day
your father died. Felt subhuman. But, your best friend

forgot her own anniversary, her husband didn't leave but wanted
to, and your oldest daughter walked down the stairs into

a mother's day celebration, left quickly, returning later
with a card made from whatever materials were available

in her cloistered room—a row of flowers, pink and orange,
only, construction paper faded by edgy winter sun. She said

she was planning to skip father's day too, no offense. Lately
you can barely remember Greece, how the wind came into

the harbor, how your body swore never to leave. The airplane
that carried you away was pure fiction. Someone else said

she couldn't remember how many lovers she'd had, but her health
was holding up so she didn't worry about amnesia, though

others now make the lover list in terror, the phone calls
made with honor though the mortal news is the newest version

of the telegram edged in black. Someone kind said it was late
October, don't you remember you're always in despair right

before November? No, I don't remember that. No one can
remember where they put their winter hats or gloves, we can't

find the Frosty the Snowman mittens that make winter acceptable,
we can't remember who wrote Canada's national anthem, can't

remember all the words though the melody stays clear. On
Bishop's desert island Crusoe holds a fragment of poetry in his

fragile mind, he may look it up years later, and Mungoshi's line, "If
you don't stay bitter and angry for too long . . ." what? If I

don't, then . . . and I don't, not for too long. It was never about
bitterness, or crossing the boundary of the page, it wasn't

about my father or my family, or the memorable dates that slip
from the angelic calendar, bereft of the idea of sanctuary,

what they meant now meaningless. The plague was different,
mortal terror of a muted sort, a privileged horror,

terrible vacancies though no one seemed to be dying.


*after Charles Baxter,*
*after Garcia-Márquez*

# How I Walk

I walk with my keys inserted
　　between each space
in my hand. I use only two
　　keys in my real life
but keep two from some past lives
　　I've led so I can have
all four spaces filled.

　　　I lace my keys between the fingers
　　　　of my left hand, my power
　　hand, the hand strong from writing,
　　　　the hand strong because it's
　　connected to my strongest arm, strong
　　　　left arm that's carried my babies.

So now I'm walking. Can you see me?
　　I am a big woman, and I walk fast.
If you look closely you can see the glint
　　of the tips of my keys. It's a flash,
not like a diamond. I don't have diamonds;
　　it's four flashes: light　　　light

light     light. When I come home from walking
    my fist is cramped from keeping
the tips of my keys at attention.

        I'm older now, have too many jobs,
            I don't walk four miles a day any more.
        When I walk now all I see are dogs
            connected to women by metal chains,
        leather chains, so really I think of them
            as dog-chained-women, or maybe women-
        chained-dogs. I no longer reach out
            my hand, palm up, to any dog,
        the women have told me they do not want
            their dogs to make friends
        with strangers. These women tied to dogs
            are all sizes. Some are tall as I am,
        some taller, some have warrior faces,
            some cupid faces, some have lines
        putting new faces on top of old faces,
            some are shockingly beautiful,
        some are tiny.

Tiny women connected to dogs
    always made sense to me.
These tiny women are vulnerable,
    I thought, so many years
ago. I thought, tiny women must be
    frightened. I have always
had, in my circle of women, tiny
    women friends. Tiny meaning:
perfect, to me, a big woman. One
    small friend of mine just

wrote a brilliant essay about walking
    in a woman's body; one dearest
small friend, raped years ago,
    no dog in the apartment
to take the knife in her place.

        Whenever I walk with that friend
            I've always thought,
        she is safe with me. I am big and walk
            with extraordinary purpose.
        If someone came toward us with menace
            as we walked the circle of
        the lake, I know I would kill that person,
            would hurl my key hand into
        his eye, his delicate throat, and I would
            tell my friend to run to the
        nearest tree and climb it and I would find
            her in the branches, my keys would
        be bloody, my hand damaged but still full
            of power.

I walk with my keys and pretend
    they give me all I need.
I pretend because I have size I will
    always be safe. Some friends
of mine who are small have never
    been attacked. Some friends
of mine, my size, have been raped and beaten.
    If I think about this I might
stop walking. And I was not there
    to save my friend the night
she was cut and raped. I have not been able
    to save friends, children, strangers.

How I walk is with my keys, alone
　　or with a friend, I walk
full of vengeance and denial, I walk
　　in fear where once I walked
in poetry, in love, in the light
　　of the blessed sun, the blessed moon.

# Cordelia: One Portrait at a Time

In a faded velvet chair holding Cordelia.
She is drowsy, giving up her madcap stomp,
barely awake, small river of milk
pulled into her belly by her rose mouth.

In a faded velvet chair holding Cordelia
the bottle goes from white to transparent,
the air bubbles remind me of the ocean,
the lonely tourists going down, the trace
of breath they give away in their dying.

In a faded velvet chair holding Cordelia.
Her eyelashes drop, the fringe of black,
small gates brushing shut, and her body
sinks deeper into my body, we wait,

and in a faded velvet chair holding Cordelia
I finally shift and rise, her blanket
sweeps behind us, robe, wedding veil,
wave and murmur, asleep and alive she breathes.

GOOD HEART

# What It Was Like Today:
# Given Over

Dickinson's vermilion wheels cruised down Saturday's street.
Bloody, scarlet, incarnadine, (yes—all those years ago—
Held up to be mocked—just another way to the top of the
    pyramid—
Though young I understood—kept going—determined dog
Posed next to sleek panther—I made some kind of peace)
Down the street they circled as all the trees gave up their crowns
As homage to the southern wind.

No one except the baby in the corner house
Expected anything but what was seen and heard.
Every October the same October, all calendars
Without a kind of essential meaning. And the baby,
The baby slept, small face turned to an open window
Full of golden wind.

# Travel

*Behold how great a territory I have explored in my*
*memory seeking thee, O Lord!*

St. Augustine, *Confessions*

Finding you everywhere      nowhere I travel
In this spaciousness are you absent.

Finding you nowhere      I know remains
My fault      inside human time      my sight

Impaired, splintered      in half-light
Half dark in the spacious hall of memory

God's watch ticks and thrums      half metal
Half bird      the watch I want its      gold chain

Clipped to the loop      my imaginary grandfather
Drunk only on God      how he loved the watch

Of God      in the spacious room of memory
God hums      *"they're writing songs of love*

*But not for me"*      how like a diva a blue jay
A crow his hum presses against the walls

In memory's room     how I ever thought
He was absent     just to make the beautiful

Men who tried to raise me feel compassion
Toward me?     Oh, no, not only for that

But in the halls of memory     God's hands
And voice     the way he is bird and prayer

Song coming from inside the closet     how he
Is everywhere     yes     I see that now

As the miniature leather books     holy
And carried     hum now in my hands

No war     no dead children     spacious hall
Of memory     room of memory     place

Where God's watch keeps all the time
How to not love him     when so completely

Not Hazel not Colette not Augusta not Paula
Not Camille not Alice not Evie not

In the spaciousness of my memory     the creek
Carries the dead girl     the living girl

And so far into my time     I still do not
Understand his choice of one     not the other

And so I travel.

# After D.H. Lawrence

Died, it took a long time
For someone to love
Trees as much as he did.

It took a long time for
The larch to stop its mourning,
For the little variegated elder
To snap out of it, grow up
Into the sky.

The copper beech felt sick,
Totally sick, made vain
By Lawrence he could not
Become humble again for
Fifty years.

Arbor day became a sham,
No one taught the children
To love the trees they planted
So the trees were on their own,
Roots stamped down by little feet,
A placid circle of cocoa shells
Around the trunk sending up
A scent the trees could not place.

D. H. Lawrence was so tormented
In his humanness he gave all
Holiness and wisdom to the trees,
And the trees accepted—which of them
Might have resisted such honor
From such tangled genius?

Slowly we learned to love trees again,
As the century closed its heart to us.

Slowly we stroke the bark, drive
A benign stake into the elm, pump
The medicine in, slowly we learn
To feed the birds so they will stay,
Make their homes in trees we tend
As the planet shudders.

Trees. We want their beautiful
Breath on our skin.

# What It Was Like Today:
# Not Taking Their Place

*You cannot speak of the deprivation of someone*
*else as if it is something that happened to you,*
*something you own. . . . You cannot speak for*
*others, he thought. You cannot take their place.*
John Yau, "Photographs for<br>an Album (Second Version)"

She'd been good at it once. Told
Be other, she could do it. Told
Be the light on the water, she was lit.
Told be the sufferer, practicing under
The latticework of ropes, done.
Every day now, though, for years,
Told to back off, she'd backed. Told
To not take the place, the space
Of any other, she did not. Kept
Margins clear, borders closed,
Nerve-ends only slightly flashed
And flared when her own sorrows
Leaked. A rebuilt engine, she
Handles the road well, the immeasurable
Losses part of the machinery now,
And the landscape still unusual,
Still riveting, still worth defending.

# THE PAINTING OF
# THE AMARYLLIS

For seven days she put off beginning
Her painting of the amaryllis.
The night before the eighth day
She dreamt she and her youngest daughter
Walked to the end of a wooden dock,
The daughter ready to swim, but she said: No.
There's a body floating there.

The corpse floated facedown to see the small fish,
The tiny snails caught in silt, and the mother
Walked into the water, pulled the body
Out by its feet, noting the woman's body
Wore a nightgown like her own.

She dragged the body to the muddy edge of the lake,
Pulled the nightgown over flesh she knew well.
The body turned on its side and the daughter sat
Between the mother and the body of the mother.

The arm of the dead woman draped over the little girl
And the living mother pulled her daughter away—
Don't let her hold you, she said, though it was terrible

To deny her dead self in this way. So they sat, the daughter
Between her two mothers and it was a horror to see
The three.

She did not paint her still life of the amaryllis
The next day. Could not carry the flower upstairs,
Could not find paper, watercolors, enough light.

When the amaryllis died back the color of the petals
Did not dispel. Unlike the skin of her dead self
These flowers still reveled in what had been
Their glory,

She threw the nightgown away,
Mourned her own death quickly and thoroughly.

The daughter grew in beauty.
Dreamt her own secrets
And loved the mother by her side.

# Aerial View of Caribou/ Slow Moves in the Black-and-White Movie

*For Stephen*

I was in the sand outside the house facing east.
The house was only a stage set, I could feel the wooden floor
under the sand, but the water was real, deep and I know
we lived there. I went with you because you told me to.
There were other people—you were part of something,
not a tour, not a vacation. You didn't know me
but I went with you. All of this was in blinding
color, we kept stopping because we were sick with longing,
had to step behind doors, to the side of wooden stairs,
we were ill with this need, and it was day for a long time
even though the words won't make it as it was, I am saying
it anyway. Then in the black-and-white movie we moved
inside the sky looking down and saw in gray dusk the caribou
move in terrible shaped tension, in slowness       in groups
and the grainy quality of the air losing light filled the train
we were in and, compelled, we looked down into the deep
snow and watched the caribou make their patterns       they
     might
be starving I thought       I said       but they looked all right and
     finally
we couldn't see through the air anymore. We didn't know
why we had to live this way.

# I KNEW HER ONCE

*She prays now to the smallest thing*
*Under the black brocade of pines,*
*She prays for the wind muffled in them,*
*For the fields in the shimmer of butterflies,*
*For valerian, dianthus, columbine,*
*She prays to pray, but cannot start.*

JEAN GARRIGUE, "STUDIES FOR AN ACTRESS"

I knew her well, and once, and long ago.
I knew her beautiful, wise, and angry,
Knew her warm and kind and right,
Knew her wrong and sorry and still.

I knew her young, and nothing's changed,
Knew her small, a bird, a shipwrecked thing.
I knew her well and not so well,
Knew her broken as glass, strong as wind.

I knew her holy, drenched and white,
Knew what prayers she finally said.
I knew her when sky was only sky
Knew when her nerve flared and fled.

*She prays now to the smallest thing.*
I never see her anymore. Knew her well
And not so well, knew the pines and columbine,
I knew enough to leave her there.

# In Emerald

*For Cordelia Seidel and Annemarie Barrett*

In Emerald all the seasons look good.
The hand-painted wooden sign lets us
Know where Emerald begins.

Everything feels better in Emerald.
Our beloved orange cat is buried
In Emerald. His cross has fallen
In winter wind, but in spring
His flowers will bloom again
And his zany spirit swirls above
Emerald, but not too high.

In Emerald there's a blue bucket
For you to eat from, and a red one
For me. There's old wooden spoons
And a sturdy chair that lives in rain
And snow and never falters.

Why did they make Emerald?
Why does this small country
Bring peace to all who enter?
Why do girls with powerful,
Tender hearts know to leave
Their homes, their parkways

And avenues and streets and
Swear allegiance to this new,
Green and growing government?

When they are at school I go
To Emerald. I never sit down,
I stand under the beautiful sign
That sways from the lilac branch,
And pray for this little country
And the girls who made it real.

# THE WIND

*What have I thought of love?*
*I have said, "It is beauty and sorrow."*
*I have thought that it would bring me lost delights,*
    *and splendor*
*As a wind out of old time. . . .*
                    LOUISE BOGAN, "BETROTHED"

And Michael Burkard said, "The wind isn't loving anyone." And
    though
I loved the poem, and though "Betrothed" can make me cry (all
    that terrible
Difference between *said* and *thought*) at all those lost from my
    life

All I really know is the wind (now and then and every day and
    night
My whole life) does love me, a most faithful, constant lover,
    whom
I write for in every book, who, when gone, I long for, who
    returns

And returns again, loves, some days with rapture, some days
Merely methodical, taking down the leaves out of duty, but in
My lifetime has refused to die for love (I know) of me.

# HOPE

*. . . it is this threatened thought that guides us from*
    *book to book, from wager to wager . . .*
*God luxuriates in the vulnerability of this thought.*
         EDMOND JABÈS, *The Book of*
            *Resemblance*, VOL. 2

## I

In the photo the purity of her hope. She's with the man she
    loves,
Her best friend slightly in front of her, leaning into the man's
    body.

They are both pure now. One has a father, a drunk, who when
    most
Deeply drunk quotes scripture, claims the towering vodka
    authority

Over all he surveys—just a girl, a woman with red hair, a small
    living
Room, shelves filled with books that are shouting at the girl—

Go to your room. Stay in the southern wind blowing on you through
    through
Your open window. They were both pure then. One has a father

Hidden in a golden attic, his holy books *clicking*     *clicking*
    with their
Brightly colored Mary Baker Eddy tabs, color-coded references

*Clicking clacking* in the attic filled with gold—the healer aloft
And in a kind of paradise, stairs that folded and closed up behind

Him as he ascended. These two gods, and the powerful mothers
Who ruled the other kingdom. In the photograph of purity

Of their hope. Perhaps they are both with the man they love.
    His
Silky white beard might touch them, his red velvet arms and
    shoulders

Thrill them. They ask for so little they always receive it. So they
    believe.
Their purity is hopeful. Their faces of hope belong to them. Still.

II

*Or rather, it is necessary to write about the same old things*
*In the same way, repeating the same things over and over*
*For love to continue and be gradually*

*Different.* In John Ashbery's "Late Echo" resides permission. It is
    good to honor a man

Who would never answer my letters of appreciation and praise.
    This is important

Reinforcement—love the artist, always, before the person. Then
    a few people
Arrive and decades slide by or maybe just a set of years, and love
    becomes

The transparent answer, almost always available, worth feeling.
    Artists or not,
They seem to be your assigned humans, hardly any cloistered
    space available,

And you know it is only right to align yourself with the parent
    who chose to stay alive.
But Muriel Rukeyser puts her beautiful mouth to my ear, says,
    *Black in morning*

*Dark, the sky going blue,*
*The river going blue.*
*Moving toward new form I am—*
*Carry again*
*All the old gifts and wars.* You can see hope in that. In the

Blue, and in the river. The new form can carry gifts and wars.
    Like my braver
Sisters and brothers, like my more frightened brothers and sisters
    I too can believe

My self endangered, just thinking there's something I MUST say
    makes me a fool

Of hope. Robert Duncan said, *Working in words I am an escapist;*
    *. . . But I want every part*

*of the actual world involved in my escape.* How I accuse myself: let
    the world
Be the world—no necessity for the *made thing*—no need for
    another word from you.

The tombstone my parents share is quiet and gray. I will never
    go there.
The actual world, hopeful, or else there would be nothing made,
    the sky,

The river, the eagles back from their graves, the great blue
    heron standing in
For my mother at the furthest back curve of her creek, the old-
    est crane

In the world, standing watch in Captiva, one leg gone, but still
    he stands
And decides, the pelicans, wide-eyed and hungry, hitting the
    water at speeds

That make them blind, but not for a while, not until they've
    eaten their fill.
Bob's mother, my mother, telling us: You might be prisoners one
    day—

Memorize poems. Read books slowly. When you are prisoners,
    these words

Will bring you hope of rescue. The actual world involved in our
　　escape.

That trail of language birds refuse to eat. So we follow it home,
　　and both
The weak and the powerful parents are gone. *For love to continue*

*And be gradually different,* they had to go away. To *carry again*
*All the old gifts and wars,* they had to be on their way. Oh, the
　　ambition

Of their deaths inspires. Let their shrines stay visible in the
　　actual world.

# Good Heart

### I

As insult it suffices.

### II

As compliment
Has a ruthless,
Snakelike charm.

### III

Some people's voices:
The tinge of exasperated love,
Was it love?
The tinge: oh, your mother's heart . . .
Voice trails off
As context erupts:
Picked up the homeless
Always late for meetings
Always let my drunken father move back home
Always thought the Red Cross might help
Her collection of strays

But no, so . . .
The backroom filled and emptied
Filled and emptied.
Did they hate her for her good heart?
Oh, no, nobody hates good hearts.

## I V

And the reviewer: "she almost always turns away
From the darkness." I have softened her words, of course.
And I am she. So I re-read my books: suicide, death by cancer,
The terrible zero at the heart of love affairs,
Viet Nam, my friend with no leg, brains on the garage wall,
The friend who leaves because of my perfect whiteness,
My disgusting lack of color and fame, the other friend,
How we acquiesce to his powerful No and speak no more,
The Junta in Greece, friends I never see again, the absence
Of god, drought, children murdered, lives given up for others
Without any sense of holiness, of valor.
Yes, I never, hardly ever, turn to darkness.
No doubt because of my fantastically evasive good heart.

## V

A simple heart is not the same
As a good heart. For one thing,
There's no parrot. Just kidding.
A good heart responds when
The goodness it was trained for
Is sent the secret, good-heart
Signal. Flaubert preferred
The simple, my mother the good.

## VI

Certain people with bad hearts
Need a certain number of people
With good hearts to buoy them up.

Certain people with bad hearts
Need to teach the ones with good hearts
To cringe, to drink the bitter draught
Of shame.

Who was that beautiful friend of mine?
The one who said, "Just say, no thanks,
I already had my dose of shame today."
I remember she told me, walk away,
Get away, even if the sentence isn't complete.
My mother turns, just slightly, in her grave.
It hurts her so much when I walk away
From cruelty.

*VII*

When I think of other cultures
I might have rested in, the ones
Where to eat the good heart
Of someone good was the right
And only thing to do, when I think
Of other lives I might have had
I can never remember if the good
Heart was beating, or had just stopped.

## VIII

As Jim said, "Your good heart
Is just blood in the water, honey."

## IX

I think of Atwood, falling in love
With her heart in its weakness,
Its mortal tremors.
Oh, the good heart, the colors of salvia
And salmon, certain azaleas, impatiens.
The good heart, its desperate longing
To defend itself, to win the good heart
Marathon, then to stutter, to shimmer,
To stop.

# When Men Poets You Admire and Respect Can Only Answer Sappho When Asked in Public Are There Any Women Poets They Admire

Sometimes they say Elizabeth Bishop. Anne Bradstreet.
Always Sappho.

Do they love fragments? Do they believe those fragments
Are symbols of a broken woman, not broken text?

Does anyone ever tell them how ruthless, how rude, how like
An unerring knife wound their answer feels as it enters the minds

Of all the living women poets listening to this answer over and over
After thirty years, forty years, so many years of teaching
And honoring these living men poets?

I hear some of my sisters laughing now. They don't mean to be mean,
Just can't believe how many poems I had to write to get to this one,

The one that's not really a poem. Oh, Sappho, intervene, intervene,
Surround these words with bracketed silence/bracketed silence/[     ]

# What It Was Like Today: Facing East

The police were after someone wicked, someone drunk,
Someone merely wrong. Their cherry red lights swiveled
Wildly in the before-sunrise plum sky of dawn. In my own
Morning innocence I squandered some time I felt I didn't have,
I let myself hear the cops rush far away from me, let myself
Have not just dawn but sunrise, too. Finally I was back
In the house, and closed all the books with great regard
And care. Before my time was up I watched the sun
Insist, watched clouds give way, felt the engine driving
My day grip, engage, turn me the other way.

# THE LAST LION

*With gratitude to Bonus Zimunya*

The last lion
Was still golden
Was still on
The move
Was still
Remarkable
With his sun-
Ray mane
His paws
Like sullen
Amber dropping
Into dust
Was still loud
And precise with
His roar
Still sleepy
With his yawn
His yellow teeth
Like an interior
Necklace
Was still
Beautiful in all

The ways we
Believe lions
Are beautiful
But he was
The last lion.

# His Red Chair

A throne, really. I think we all agreed on that.
Arriving home to find it on fire, his cigarette
Pushing deep into the arm of the red chair,
With red flames to match, and he, asleep,
Not good sleep, that other kind, and we
Decided to save him, I guess, his arm seared,
His soft flannel shirt felt baked, yes, as if
Done, ready to come from the oven, so we
Lifted him, though not gently, saving is saving
And gentle is gentle, I think we sort of carried
Him to the lawn, then I went back inside,
Poured cool water onto the red chair, the flames,
Kept pouring water down into the deep recesses
Of the arm of the chair as if the chair was very
Very thirsty, and so was I, from saving him,
And from saving the chair, too, very thirsty.

# The Exchange

*For Jean Adams*

The tone of our exchanges: flat     tired     luminous
    charged     broken
Built     ragged     Made     every day from our devotion
    Make a friend

Ship visible     one quarter of a century     is that enough time
Twenty-five years of walking     just a couple of beautiful
    spiders

Making the daily strand of language     threadbare
    radiant oh     we
Have been the lucky ones     all narrative strategies     all
    poetics used

Never used up     in one three-dimensional quarter of a
    century all those
Shining children     human riddles     precious library of souls
    words

No words     words again     did we ever understand the
    edifice created?
Are creating     a made thing

# Signing My Name in the Book of the Dead

*For my sister-in-law, Mary Seidel*

Was an accident. I simply saw the book at a Catholic funeral
    and wrote
My name—cell memory of a Protestant girlhood. The smallest
    parish

In St. Paul listens now as my name is added; they may be bewil-
    dered about
Where the name came from, but they will pray for me and I
    know enough

To be honored—this will happen, as surely as I know too many
    good men
Die too soon, too young, as surely as I know my beautiful crows
    are killing

The gleaming cardinals I admire. I've told my friends this
    year—I'm just
Trying to live as if I am dying. And then I just don't. The
    spiritual buzz

From this decision works most days. Lately, though, I see myself

As a small queen of prophecy, mostly low-key prophet thoughts,
    no crown

Involved, but I have been attuned, afraid to say aloud a fear
    about a friend,
Afraid I have predicted too often my own quiet little death. I
    signed the book

Of the dead at Dee's funeral. I thought I was saying to Dave and
    Mary,
"I'm here. Thinking of you." It was just another miserable
    November day

With enough sorrow to go around. I don't understand the book
    of the dead
Or why Carol's husband, Dianne's husband, had to go too soon.
    The leader

Of the crow family got murdered this past summer in my
    neighborhood.
Beautiful and headless he lay on Henry's lawn, and children
    from the block

Came day after day, lay flowers on his shining body until just one
    edge of wing
Tip showed. I can't bear all the dead some days. At the funeral
    Dan and Lisa

And Eric and I held hands. Everything felt too sad. I felt my own
    dead mother
And father might be sitting in another pew, too far from my
    attention.

Now I can't stop living as if I am dying. I started about eighteen
    months ago
Thinking I was, dying I mean, but I wasn't. It's been a peaceful
    human choice—

The kind I seldom make. I think of all who are gone and live in
    their honor.

# GONE

*The pelicans are all gone. A few other things have*
*changed—I'm shocked, constantly in a state of shock—*
*perhaps that should be my epitaph—she's shocked to be*
*dead, really . . .*
PATRICIA WEAVER FRANCISCO

Shocking to be gone, though
When pelicans go, who really
Wants to stay? Cormorant
And albatross, one-eyed
Pirates clinging to the mast,
Gone, too. Too late for finding
Treasure, that's shocking, too,
And too late to be rich, gone,
The meaning or value of what
It could be; too late, too gone
Down the path to see oneself
Young in any mirror; gone, can't
Tell my children anymore: love
This, and this, hate this, make this—
Gone from the beautiful canals
Of their ears. Gone, the rope swing
Forty feet high, ridiculous in its
Absence, gone, anyone smart enough

To not take down a rope swing; gone,
Shockingly gone, some of my bitterness,
And terrible and true, gone some hatred
That kept me safe. Gone, the epitaphs
So happily written, in the gone days
When I would never die.

# REM CHANNELS LEONARD COHEN

The voice in my dream said,
Now that you are close to death
You must. . . .
This is what I hate about dream voices.

Definitely past the middle of my life
(I've always assumed I would die
At the age my father killed himself—
Just a few more years left to get it right)

Definitely past the middle though the music
Still pounds inside my car
And then I heard them sound like Cohen
And felt another circle close,
The golden clasp of reverence and authority
Link the golden clasp of homage and voice
And the click, the circle secured, the affectless
Voices paying honor and I was seventeen,
Of course I was (you say, didn't you promise
No more of the personal?) I was seventeen,
Nearly dead of carbon monoxide fumes,
Sleeping in the kitchen of my Greek boyfriend's

Restaurant, beautiful sleep of almost death
And Leonard Cohen's voice intruded,
Mixing with the poison, diluting the poison
Just enough so I could wake
My beloved friend, could stagger
From the kitchen holding her,
And we vomited over and over
Into the beautiful grass of Corfu,
Waves pounding just one hundred yards
Away, well, I was alive, and it seemed
To matter, and Leonard Cohen's voice
Welcomed me back to the life
I'd almost lost.

In my car the circle closed.

# COMMON

*For Aisling Virginia and her parents*

Closest relation to crow.
Common. Conspicuous.
In open country. In open
Country I reside, but Magpie
Eludes. Plenty of trees
Strong enough for their
Huge hodgepodge nests
But they are west. Where
I am not. Or rarely. In
Beautiful twilight air
Before the sun rose I
Held Aisling Virginia
By the kitchen window
And Blackbilled Magpie
Draped his streaming tail
As he perched on a tree
So near to us—in dim
Early light my eyes skimmed
The open country, saw
My first magpie, startled
And happy I lifted the baby
And said the common word,
Bird, not knowing who
Until later I found him
In a book. I remember

The rooks who guarded
My bedroom window
In Scotland, all those years
Ago, waiting for my first
Child, whose child I hold
Now, in magpie country.
The book says their call
Can be a rapid series of
Large, harsh notes, or an
Ascending whine, says
Their song lasts too long,
Is poor and raucous, but
I don't mind, don't even
Agree. Jays, magpies,
Beautiful black crows.
They are family Corvidae
But I won't remember.
I live with jays and crows
And no one knows better
Than me how to love them.
Now I love magpies, too,
Though not as I love Aisling,
Folded in the arms of her
Parents in open country,
The first nest, made, as
Bachelard's robin did, with
The steady force of their
Heartbeats shaping the circle
She can live in until she
Flies. Magpie, the book says
You wander erratically in winter.
If it's true, I'll watch for you.

# Time and Love

*There'll be time enough for rocking*
*when we're old*
*We can rock all day*
*in rocking chairs of gold*
*But tonight I think*
*I'd rather just go dancing . . .*

STEPHIN MERRITT, "TIME ENOUGH
FOR ROCKING WHEN WE'RE OLD"

Laura Nyro was there, and in the dream the men liked her voice, too. She called our names and we went up on the roof. In the true story of time and love I was so young, and in the dream, not so much. This double perspective helped me survive, I see that now. My survival was written in dream language projected onto the brick wall that wouldn't stop anyone from jumping if they needed to. Lou Reed was there, miles and years away from being smart enough to love Laurie Anderson, and we decided not to be like anyone on the roof, even though they were all so beautiful and their souls were naked and their drugged eyes stunned with beauty of windows. We were from there, otherwise how would we have known about the party? We were essentially from there, but there were Greyhound buses in our past, and we were the kind of people who tended to believe in things. Whatever we had believed in hadn't crushed us yet, which is why we kept our clothes on, why we huddled in the

corner and put our hands up when the man who was filming
it all came toward us. We knew we had plenty of time, all the
time we wanted, and so we danced. Our wild dancing such a
comfort and joy, even the emaciated ones, needles sliding into
their arms, even the cool and crowned, the crazed careerists and
hangers-on, they all took a break from their real lives on the roof
and watched us, without hatred or dismissal, and Laura danced
too, her purple scarf signaling no surrender, no surrender. We
never stopped dancing. This is how it happened in the true
dream of time and love.

# The Park

*For Larry Wells Bowman, Daniel Clifford Bowman,*
*And in memory of Virginia Bowman, 1911 — 1997*

*And I went alone, and I did not mind,*
*Not thinking of you as left behind.*
            Thomas Hardy, "The Walk"


## I


My love for our park, its hidden valley, its perfect creek,
Its secret places for great blue herons, tiny river otters,
The watercress still waiting for the girl I was, jumping
The barbed wire fence, aiming for the beautiful green
Leaves my mother used to send me to gather for lunch.

My passion for its secret paths, for its wild mix of oak,
Maple, pine, cedar, chokecherry, mulberry, sandcherry,
Blue flax and coneflowers, butterfly weed streaking
The hillside with oranges and golds anyone might love,
My happiness as the new islands in the creek bed

Rise up to replace and remind me of the islands of
Childhood, always the orphan running from some kind
Of human villainy, crossing the creek to make my home
On any island left behind after the spring floods finished
Their work re-carving the curves and angles in bright blues and
    rusts.

Kristine's voice calling from her side of the small valley;
How we suffered saying good-bye, how we called back
And forth, all the while knew we would find each other
The next day; and the winters when the creek would freeze
And no snow would fall—we could skate for miles

On these beautiful curves of ice, one day winning the Olympics,
The next escaping from some fairy-tale plot flamed into danger
So we had reason to skate faster, farther. The shattering sled
Rides from tops of both hills, how much ideal danger we sought
And survived, our brothers never cruel, never stopped us.

## II

My mother's park. That's what I call it still. Hardy's words
On the third anniversary of her death made me cry, my whole
    poem
Feels kind of hunched over, a protective posture around what I
    love,
Around whom I love, but inside the protection trying too hard
    to let
Sentiment *be*, I hold the silver knives, I'm ready for murder,

And no one who really knows me is surprised. My hands still feel
The grips of her wheelchair, my back still feels the small weight
    of her,
Suddenly always in front of me, winning every race sitting down.
    I see
My brothers taking turns pushing her along the brilliant paths of
    our
Family's history. Take a left, the luna moths are waiting. Take a
    right,

Is that our father, blessedly still and sober on the small wooden
    bridge?
My beautiful brothers walk next to me, every time I'm there,
    alone
Or with Stephen, Cordelia, Joe, Molly, Brendan. I already walk
    there
With Sarah, with Aisling, my mother back from her death,
    walking
With us, holding Aisling's small hand, none of us left behind.

# KINGDOMS

# IF YOU SAY LUCK
# YOU CAN'T SAY GOD

You said *God* and *luck* and you can't.
Even on TV where people say anything
You can't.

And you said God and there's no such thing
As luck.
You shouldn't have said that either.

And you said *luck*, and *blessed*, and *survive*
And it was all right that you were speaking.

You others—someone like me will tear
Your mouths away from your faces.

You said *God* and *luck* and I shot out the TV
Screen and the glass was glass and shattered.

And you said God, no luck at all, and I
Attacked the outlet, the short black cord,
The lethal prongs.

Don't talk about God. Shut up.
And you, the one who said *luck* and *blessed*
And *survive*. You can shut up, too,
But you can keep your face, and your mouth
For kissing.

# Portrait of Soon

*Perhaps the earth can teach us*
*As when everything seems dead in winter*
*And later proves to be alive.*

PABLO NERUDA, "KEEPING QUIET"

Raccoons wrap their claws
In gauze, quiet as they cross
Linoleum, open the refrigerator,
Take only the fresh fruit,
The best vegetables.
Safely back in their winter
Forest they fling the gauze
Skyward, decorate the sleeping
Oaks, streamers calm and white.

The peony roots keep secret,
Avoid the crazy neighbor
With the rototiller, roots
Plunge straight down, commit
To another spring, to giant
White blooms streaked
With nature's quiet bloodlines.

The last one hundred tigers hold
Private meetings, plan the screaming
Deaths of zebras, decide to fight to stay
A part of this noisy planet, whomever
They must kill.

# Two Sisters

There are two sisters.
One is more pleasant.
One wears skirts that swirl
Confectionary
And abrupt. One liked,
One not. Their value
Is, as Benjamin said,
Ivy wrapped a-
Round the ruin of
Their stories which we
Will never know. One
Is changing, one is
Not. One is not me,
One is not even
You. Sadly, this is
No riddle, and no
Tragedy that any
One might notice
Who pretends to care
About two sisters,
One gone on ahead,
One dressed and swirling.

# The Boy I Quit For

He's lovely, handsome, really.
When he arrived he had sunlight-
White hair, rococo curls, gray blue
Eyes oceanic and peering.

Now his hair's dark, straight, he's
Slender as reeds, slender as a mirror,
And smells of dense tobacco, of
Cigarette packs and ashtrays
From Toronto and Biscayne Bay.

When he arrived before dawn,
Serious and ours, I resolved to
Stop smoking—no other choice,
Really, with his skin smelling
Of angel and air, of soap and
Pure white cotton towels—no way
To keep the vice that kept me slim
And gave me such filtered pleasure.

Then I started again, not til he was
Two or so, then finally stopped, and
Sent him a letter. Dear J., I wrote,

You're the boy I quit for, in honor
Of life and love, wisdom and willpower.
I quit for you, because it's right
That I should. I suffered the required
Length of time, and moved on, and
He moved on, moved out, and he's
Lovely, handsome, really, with
Gray blue eyes and he moves
With grace through smoke
And I see him clearly though
I can barely see him.

# July // The Right Hand Was a Medusa

*For Juliet*

The head, too. And the grief. And the children gone.

The door opened, and truly, a shaft of light intruded.
The door opened, and we should never have looked.

Curious women. We always were.
Someone told us it was a value.

Someone we didn't care for told us
To stop being curious, so we knew we were right.

So, though we are held now, timeless and
Out of luck, out of time, we were once in sunlight.

What Medusa meant changed and changed again.
Our luck and grief transformed, truly, we could
Imagine alchemy like that.

This took care of ten percent of the grief.

And that we were together, not alone.

# August // No Rain

Still summer, and on the steps of the museum
Poseurs and the arrogant gather in honor of art.

Your head was on fire—they couldn't let you in—
Those flames too weird and meaningful

Might touch off a golden storm inside the Monet.
Or not. You never, never know about art and money.

You never know about money and fire,
Their curious marriage, their rapture.

Nobody was drunk, though. I think the heat
Just makes people pray for rain that doesn't

Arrive. Nobody's drinking, nobody's cooking.
Too many people are forgetting they hate winter.

I'm not, though. I hate winter. And today,
I'm so uneasy standing near the rich.

I know it's not their fault they live under
The money tree, I know how hard it is for them

When the poor refuse to love art, refuse to pose
On the steps of the museum. Today

In the brilliant heat I would burn their money
And dip my brush into the cinders for art's sake.

# BLUE HERON

We arrived carrying our usual human trouble, hoping to walk
Those troubles deep into the forest, hoping
To leave them there. Not as burden for the forest, knowing
All too well the forest and its beautiful indifference.

At the dam I looked left to a hidden curve of creek,
Joe looked right to the still water past the small island.
Blue Heron lifted from the curve, her wingspan almost
Touched us, and she landed past the island, bowed to eat.

Right after my mother died, eight years ago, I saw Blue Heron
In this small valley; I knew then my mother had left
Her exhausted body behind and slipped into this
Winged disguise. I was happy for my mother's new life.

We've searched these eight years for one more sight
Of Blue Heron. And in our sorrows this day, three times
We saw her take flight, three times land, three times lean
Into shallow water for food and reflection. *She's gone,*

I said to Joe. We carried the sight of her back to our city,
Our hearts strangely stirred and strangely at peace,
Her extended wings visible against the green of spring.

# The Four Goldfinches and One Scarlet Tanager

At the eastern edge, bisque and caramel dunes
At the eastern edge, scrub oak and pine

Two mornings walking, the goldfinches
Making their inverted arcs, two by two

Shaping the yellow line of sun's fire
Shaping the undercurves of daffodil cups

So quick, so brilliantly yellow and small
So sure as they stitched the oak and pine

Together with gold thread and tiny needles
Together they careened down the road

All four following the curve of the old
Pirate road and then gone, into the thicket

And staring in vain for them, bright morning
Companions, eyes adjusted to the shock

Of the perfect scarlet tanager, resting
On the tree they'd flown past in their escape

Darkest eye, deepest scarlet, stunned
That no one had been searching for him

Somewhere in the safety of the forest
At the edge of the dunes the four yellow

Birds repeated and repeated
their beautiful geometry.

# Small Panacea and Lucky for Us

Slight breath of wind
More wind and finally
The cloud over the cheery face
Of the sun, golden narcissist

One cigarette every three years
Or three cigarettes every one year

Love and only love, true love

The bridge in the distance
And the bridge close by

Constant misunderstanding
Of the real reasons

Being interested
In the motives of strangers

More wind, then if we're lucky
The rain falls down

Chance and luck set free
In what's left
Of wilderness

# Nine Mile Creek //
# What Was Written There

At the first curve of silt and sand:
*Buddha slept here, and well.*
And at the second: *Jesus saves.*
*Do you? Jesus loves. Do you?*
At the edge of the third swimming hole
We read: *Kali makes it live and die.*
*Do you?*

For fifty years my family's walked
In this small valley, always near
The banks, the creek water rust
And russet, metallic and gleaming.
For fifty years the secret spring's
Helped the watercress glow green
In all four seasons. Love, save,
Sleep, live and die. We answered
Yes to all, kept walking. The Blue
Heron—who is really my dead mother
Come back to us, who is really a
Blue Heron—watches over us as
We read.

# The Baby

She had a brief and beautiful greed for milk, for the color blue, for more milk, and many late-night television shows. She was constantly luminous, showily glowish, when we carried her from the prairie to the West Coast her glittering skin and eyes sustained and inspired us, though we were not pioneers.

The baby, born in winter, loves summer. The baby loves being warm, hot even. The baby lies facedown on a blue towel and dreams of reindeer who do not glow with radioactivity, dreams of lions.

And now the baby, in October, admits summer has ended. And now the baby hates us all for our powerlessness. Sick of our love, sick of being carried. Preferring her crib, her mobile of six Shetland ponies, spinning and neighing.

She was just a little wild, the baby. Her parents were a little too tame, so she got to be a little too wild. Not like a reindeer at all, much more like a tawny, ragged lion. But small. A very small, secretive kind of lion, with teeth that could hurt you. She was a small, dark gold lion right here on earth.

# INDEX OF TITLES
# AND FIRST LINES

*Poem titles are set in italics and first lines in roman, excepting*
*first lines originally set in italics, whose style is maintained here.*

The yellow house she had once agreed to live in was this one. *16*
Yes, there's reverence for his genius, the quick nod *35*
You are cutting apples for your children. *88*
You said *God* and *luck* and you can't. *249*
You thought it was only you. You couldn't remember the day *193*
your meeting at yellowstone *84*
you've seen a three foot long *93*

# ACKNOWLEDGMENTS

This long poem, *Willow Room, Green Door,* was written from June through September 1, 2005.

The section of the poem, *It's a Poem about Summer and Summer is Over,* was read at The Loft's fundraiser for the victims of Hurricane Katrina.

Guardians for this book: Shirley Jackson, Barbara Deming, Cordelia Seidel, Zach Dickson, Molly Keenan, Aaron Licktov, Larry Bowman, Daniel Bowman, André Gide, Henri Coulette, Roseann Lloyd, Jim Moore, Keith Prussing, and all others who come and go in the text.

As always, gratitude to my students. My thanks to Sandy Beach for the precise Barbara Deming poem. My thanks to K. Alma Peterson for letting me have her line, *guessed "true" answer was "bridge."* Special thanks to Stephen Seidel, Joe Seidel, Maura Rockcastle, Brendan, Sarah, and Aisling Keenan, and my aunt, Mary Seidel. Special mention and love to the two who loved the green door as I did: Mary François Rockcastle and Patricia Weaver Francisco.

DEBORAH KEENAN is the author of six collections of poetry: *Household Wounds; The Only Window That Counts; One Angel Then,* a limited edition text designed and illustrated and made by Gaylord Schanilec; *Happiness; Good Heart;* and *Kingdoms.* She is also the author, with Jim Moore, of the poetry collection *How We Missed Belgium,* and is coeditor, with Roseann Lloyd, of *Looking for Home: Women Writing About Exile,* which won an American Book Award in 1991.

Keenan has received two Bush Foundation Fellowships for her poetry, an NEA Fellowship, and the Loft-McKnight Poet of Distinction Award, among other awards and grants. In 1994, 2000, and 2004 she was named professor of the year for teaching and service in the MFA program at Hamline University.

Keenan lives with her husband, Stephen Seidel, director of Urban Programs for Habitat for Humanity International. She has four children and is a professor and faculty advisor in the Graduate Liberal Studies School at Hamline University. Keenan lives and works in beautiful, mysterious St. Paul, Minnesota.

MORE POETRY FROM

# MILKWEED ◯ EDITIONS

TO ORDER BOOKS OR FOR MORE
INFORMATION, CONTACT MILKWEED AT
(800) 520-6455 OR VISIT OUR WEBSITE
(WWW.MILKWEED.ORG).

BLUE LASH
*James Armstrong*

TURNING OVER THE EARTH
*Ralph Black*

ASTONISHING WORLD:
THE SELECTED POEMS OF ÁNGEL
GONZÁLEZ 1956—1986
*Translated from the Spanish by Steven
Ford Brown and Gutierrez Revuelta*

MORNING EARTH:
FIELD NOTES IN POETRY
*John Caddy*

THE PHOENIX GONE, THE TERRACE
EMPTY
*Marilyn Chin*

PLAYING THE BLACK PIANO
*Bill Holm*

FURIA
*Orlando Ricardo Menes*

MUSIC FOR LANDING PLANES BY
*Éireann Lorsung*

THE FREEDOM OF HISTORY
*Jim Moore*

THE PORCELAIN APES OF MOSES
MENDELSSOHN
*Jean Nordhaus*

FIREKEEPER:
SELECTED POEMS
*Pattiann Rogers*

SOME CHURCH
*David Romtvedt*

FOR MY FATHER, FALLING ASLEEP AT
SAINT MARY'S HOSPITAL
*Dennis Sampson*

ATLAS
*Katrina Vandenberg*

# MILKWEED EDITIONS

Founded in 1979, Milkweed Editions is one of the largest independent, nonprofit literary publishers in the United States. Milkweed publishes with the intention of making a humane impact on society, in the belief that good writing can transform the human heart and spirit. Within this mission, Milkweed publishes in four areas: fiction, nonfiction, poetry, and children's literature for middle-grade readers.

# JOIN US

Milkweed depends on the generosity of foundations and individuals like you, in addition to the sales of its books. In an increasingly consolidated and bottom-line-driven publishing world, your support allows us to select and publish books on the basis of their literary quality and the depth of their message. Please visit our Web site (www. milkweed.org) or contact us at (800) 520-6455 to learn more about our donor program.